For Such a Time

ED DICKERSON

Nampa, Idaho | Oshawa, Ontario, Canada
www.pacificpress.com

Cover design by Gerald Lee Monks
Cover design resources from Sermonview

Copyright © 2017 by Pacific Press® Publishing Association
Printed in the United States of America
All rights reserved

The author assumes full responsibility for the accuracy of all facts and quotations as cited in this book.

You can obtain additional copies of this book by calling toll-free 1-800-765-6955 or by visiting http://www.adventistbookcenter.com.

Unless otherwise noted, all Bible quotations are from THE HOLY BIBLE, NEW INTERNATIONAL VERSION®. Copyright © 1973, 1978, 1984, 2011 by Biblica, Inc.® Used by permission. All rights reserved worldwide.

Scripture quotations marked NKJV are from the New King James Version®. Copyright © 1982 by Thomas Nelson. Used by permission. All rights reserved.

Scripture quotations marked WEB are from the World English Bible.

Library of Congress Cataloging-in-Publication Data
Names: Dickerson, Ed (Edgar Dean), 1950- author.
Title: For such a time : chosen women of the Bible / Ed Dickerson.
Description: Nampa : Pacific Press Publishing Association, 2017.
Identifiers: LCCN 2017003884 | ISBN 9780816362912 (pbk.)
Subjects: LCSH: Women in the Bible,
Classification: LCC BS575 .D528 2017 | DDC 220.9/2082—dc23 LC record available at https://lccn.loc.gov/2017003884

March 2017

Dedication

For Shoshannah,
whose insight started me on this journey of discovery.
A wise woman whom it is my honor to call daughter.

Acknowledgments

A book is never really the product of one person. There are so many who contribute in one way or another. The women in my life, daughters Shoshannah and Elise, daughter-in-law Erica, and my wife, Mavis, have enriched my life and aided my understanding—limited though it is—of the Daughters of Eve. The Eastern Iowa Scribes Christian writers group is a continual education and encouragement. Specifically, Kristin Snodgrass and Molly Elliott, two young women, talented writers, who gave me much valuable feedback and made this a better book. I also want to thank all the fine people at Pacific Press, with special thanks to Amanda Withers whose fine touch as editor has made this a better book. And once again, I must always mention my wife, my sweetheart, my far, far better half, Mavis, without whose support I would accomplish little, and those accomplishments would mean less.

Contents

Introduction..9

Chapter 1: Matthew's Quartet...11

Chapter 2: Tamar 15

Chapter 3: Jochebed..29

Chapter 4: Rahab 38

Chapter 5: Deborah 42

Chapter 6: Ruth 49

Chapter 7: Hannah 66

Chapter 8: Abigail 72

Chapter 9: Bathsheba..80

Chapter 10: Woman of Shunem..85

Chapter 11: Esther 94

Chapter 12: Mary of Nazareth...112

Chapter 13: The Woman at the Well 116

Chapter 14: The Bleeding Woman 122

Chapter 15: The Syrophoenician Woman..................................128

Chapter 16: Mary of Bethany..131

Chapter 17: Mary of Magdala 135

Chapter 18: What These Stories Have Taught Me 138

Introduction

"Whenever women in the Bible brought their case directly to God," my daughter, Shoshannah, said to me one day, "He always ruled in their favor." Specifically, she pointed to the case of the daughters of Zelophehad, related in the book of Numbers.

While preparing to enter the land of promise, the Israelites took a census, both to determine the number of fighting men available and how many households were eligible to receive land. Zelophehad, of the tribe of Manasseh, had died in the wilderness without a son. But he had seven daughters, and they appealed to Moses. "Why should our father's name disappear from his clan because he had no son? Give us property among our father's relatives."

Moses laid their argument before the Lord, and God agreed with the women, and ordered that they be given land. These women had challenged the assumptions of their culture—quite a remarkable action. It established a precedent in Israel, but was it merely a response to a specific set of circumstances?

That episode provided evidence in favor of my daughter's position, and I could think of no examples that contradicted what she had said and several others that confirmed it. But I had learned to be cautious of the word *always*, especially when it comes to Bible study.

The Bible is a complex book, and God in His revelation of Himself and His will often surprises us and confounds our expectations. So I had learned to be thorough in my study before coming to a conclusion. I wanted to take an honest look at the question: "How did God respond when women took the lead?" Not when women did what men wished they would. Not when women did what society and culture expected of them. Not when women "knew their place," and acted only within it. No, I wanted to know how God responded to women who, "when thwarted by the male world or when they find it lacking in moral insight or practical initiative, do not hesitate to take their destiny, or the nation's, into their own hands."[1]

I did not attempt to study all the women in the Bible; I specifically wanted to know how God responded to women who seized an opportunity. So I assembled a list, eventually composed of seventeen examples of women who seized the initiative, to investigate how God responded to each one.

For the most part, I knew the names and the stories of these women, but previously I had failed to truly engage with them, to recognize the importance the biblical authors gave them. I had either minimized them—considering them footnotes to the larger story—or passed over them entirely. Only after careful re-examination did I uncover the great lengths to which the biblical authors went to emphasize the importance of these women in God's plan.

I did not utilize any new ideas or techniques. On the contrary, I employed the same methods I had learned in Seminary and through forty years of Bible study. It was just that, for the first time, I seriously examined the literary craftsmanship and content of these particular biblical stories.

In other words, I carefully took note of how the story was told, how the events were selected and arranged, the language used, and what was included or excluded. In some cases, God or someone speaking for Him passed a verdict on the woman's actions, and that made my conclusion easy. More often, and as we find often in the Bible, God expressed approval or disapproval through His actions, and that served as the basis for my evaluation.

As I began the study, what I found surprised me. The more deeply I studied, the more these stories inspired and astonished me. Far from echoing the low regard for women in their culture, the biblical writers repeatedly portrayed women as "a daunting adversary or worthy partner, quite man's equal in a moral or psychological perspective, capable of exerting just as much power as he through her intelligent resourcefulness."[2]

I began to recognize that these stories portrayed women of wisdom, of powerful prayer, of amazing faith, dynamic leadership, and prophetic insight. In fact, I began to see that they often paralleled the stories of men who were hailed as worthy servants of God. And so I began to pair these women's stories with those of men, as spiritual "strong partners."

In the pages that follow, I share this voyage of discovery. It has enlarged my understanding of Scripture and enriched my life. I hope it will do the same for you.

---

1. Robert Alter, *The Art of Biblical Narrative* (New York: Basic Books, 2011), Kindle edition, chap. 7.
2. Ibid.

ONE

Matthew's Quartet
Four Scandalous Women

But where to start?

I began with Matthew's gospel, because Matthew first drew my attention to the importance of biblical women. He begins his Gospel with the genealogy of Jesus, but it's a singular genealogy because it includes four women. That's remarkable in itself. But when you examine *who* they are, it becomes even more so. These are not just any women. Matthew does not include Sarah, Abraham's wife; nor did he include any of the first three patriarchs' wives. He does not include Eve, for his genealogy only goes back to Abraham. He does not include any of these obvious candidates. So whom did he include?

First, in this genealogy of the Messiah, Matthew mentions Tamar. Even in our day, when sexual matters are discussed quite openly, the story of Tamar—a woman who disguises herself as a prostitute and convinces her father-in-law to buy sex from her—gives us pause. It certainly must have made Matthew's audience uncomfortable!

But then he follows up with Rahab, the prostitute from Jericho. When we tell her story to children, we describe Rahab as an innkeeper. But the context and vocabulary in the book of Joshua are clear, and five other Old Testament passages refer to her as a prostitute. Rahab was *not* just an innkeeper. That occasions more discomfort.

Next, Matthew mentions Ruth. Finally, we come to a story with which we are comfortable. Well, mostly comfortable, that is, because there are parts of the story that we tone down a bit. We don't mention the strong prohibition God had given Israel against marrying foreigners, especially those from Moab. There are several reasons for this discomfort with Moab, and they are quite deserved. Now we have three women, each one of them with serious questions about why they were allowed to marry into Israel and bear a child who would become an ancestor of royalty. But Matthew has not yet finished shocking us.

It would be difficult to imagine a more scandalous woman than Bathsheba. The story of David and Bathsheba reads like a soap opera. Nudity, adultery, betrayal, conspiracy, murder—and that's just the beginning.

That is Matthew's quartet of female ancestors of Christ—four women, all with questionable pasts. This brings us back to the question, Why? Why did Matthew include these, and *only* these, women? Why does he insist on focusing our attention on these four difficult situations? Aside from being ancestors of Jesus, what do these four women have in common? After all, in forty-two generations, there had to be forty-two wives and mothers. Yet Matthew mentions only these four. What is Matthew trying to tell his readers? And why did God allow these women to become part of the royal line, and even ancestors, of Christ?

They come from different backgrounds. Three are Gentiles. One was an adulteress, another was a prostitute, and yet another pretended to be a prostitute. Indeed, persuading her own father-in-law to pay her for sex is how she became part of this genealogy! Three are widows—although one became a widow only after committing adultery, when her adulterous lover conspired to murder her first husband.

These women are anything but ordinary. They do not fit our image of the "perfect woman." They were not the timid little "fruitful vine[s] in the corner of the house"—the psalmist's idea of a good spouse. They had little in common with the "ideal woman" pictured in Proverbs 31, except for one crucial characteristic—*initiative*. They became ancestors of Christ because they seized or created an opportunity, took the initiative, and acted—often contrary to male desires and expectations. And yet God honored these women as only He could—by including them in the Messianic line.

These four women formed the starting point for my study. As we go through this roll call of heroines, we shall see again and again that the biblical authors have structured these tales in such a way as to make it clear how their experience parallels that of the significant men who played crucial roles in God's plans—such spiritual giants as Abraham, Moses, Joseph, Samuel, Solomon, Peter, Paul, and John the revelator.

Perhaps that strikes you as a little far-fetched. I understand that, and I sympathize. As I studied one woman after another the story of each one contained surprising details I had never noticed before, the evidence kept piling up. The biblical authors delight in showing us that the God of old, who performed wonders and saving actions in Israel's past, is active in their own time, and in the same way. They do this by repeating words, settings, circumstances, patterns, or sequences of events that recall the earlier episodes. All this was designed to help their audience—and eventually us—maintain and deepen our faith in God.

Some may object to the idea that human authors took so active a role in fashioning the biblical narratives. I confess that the idea that biblical authors were actively shaping what they wrote at first made me uncomfortable. When I was growing up, I thought that the biblical authors, especially the authors of the four Gospels, were essentially inspired stenographers—that they simply wrote down everything that happened. But John, in his Gospel, laid that idea to rest.

"Jesus performed many other signs in the presence of his disciples, which are not recorded in this book. But these are written that you may believe that Jesus is the Messiah, the Son of God, and that by believing you may have life in his name" (John 20:30, 31).

John not only tells us that he did not write the other signs that Jesus performed, but explains how he decided which ones to include. He selected the ones that would help us believe. Indeed, more of Jesus' actions were unrecorded than the total that were included in all the Gospels. Again, John explains: "Jesus did many other things as well. If every one of them were written down, I suppose that even the whole world would not have room for the books that would be written" (John 21:25).

John explicitly declared the purpose of his book and explains how he decided which episodes to include in it, but most of the biblical authors do not. We have to deduce their purpose and method of selection. Still, every biblical author picked and chose, including some episodes and words, and excluded others, arranging them to emphasize some details while omitting others. He repeats phrases, and he compares and contrasts characters, events, and words. He names some characters that he describes and leaves others unnamed. In scores of little ways, the author shapes his tale to communicate the wonder of how God relates to deeply flawed human beings.

Does this idea somehow diminish the role of inspiration in writing the Bible? Not at all. As Peter testified: "Prophets, though human, spoke from God as they were carried along by the Holy Spirit" (2 Peter 1:21).

The Spirit "carried the prophets along," but *they* spoke. They spoke their words, in their language, to an audience steeped in their common culture. Having been entrusted with God's message for His people, they bent every effort to effectively communicate that message. As we study these stories, we shall discover the reason Matthew included those four questionable women in Jesus' genealogy. But that is for later—when we study a fifth woman.

For now, we begin where Matthew began. We begin with the first woman in Matthew's genealogy and the first woman in Scripture who seizes the initiative and receives God's approval for doing so—even though, in this case, she does it in an unusual way, and decidedly without the permission of the man supposedly in charge of her. We begin with Tamar.

TWO

TAMAR
TRANSIENT TEMPTRESS

There are many stories in the Bible suitable for children. This is *not* one of them. In fact, this is a story adults rarely talk about with each other. At best, it's troubling. It speaks frankly about episodes and actions rarely discussed in polite company.

The entire story is found in Genesis 38, but here is a short summary of the sequence of events. Judah marries and has three sons. They grow up, and the oldest son, named Er, marries our heroine, Tamar. He dies, leaving Tamar childless. In accordance with custom, Judah gives his second son, Onan, to Tamar to give her children, who will then be raised up in the dead Er's name. But Onan reneges on his responsibility in a particularly offensive fashion, what we call *coitus interruptus*, and God kills him. Having lost two sons, Judah, now fearful for his own legacy, delays by declaring his third son, Shelah, too young to marry, and sends Tamar back to live with her father.

Time passes. During this time, Judah's wife dies, but still he does not offer Tamar relief from her predicament. When she realizes that Judah has no intention of giving her another husband, she decides to achieve through stratagem the justice she has been denied.

Disguising herself as a prostitute, Tamar purposefully encounters Judah. Not recognizing her, Judah seeks her services. He has no money to pay her but promises a goat kid to be sent later. No fool, Tamar demands that he leave personal items with her as a guarantee that the promised payment will be made. He agrees, and they, shall we say, consummate the bargain.

More time passes, and Judah sends a friend with a goat kid to where he had met the prostitute, but she cannot be found. Three more months pass, and Judah is informed that his daughter-in-law—the one without a husband—has become pregnant. He immediately insists that she suffer the extreme penalty—death by burning.

As she is being summoned for that penalty, she presents the personal items Judah had given the "prostitute" as guarantee for payment. "I am with child by the man to whom these things belong,"[1] she says. Recognizing them, Judah recognizes his guilt, and exonerates Tamar.[2]

There we have it. We find this whole episode disturbing. It combines a series of (at best) indelicate acts: *coitus interruptus*, a woman pretending to be a prostitute, a patriarch having sex with (he thinks) a prostitute, but who is in fact his twice-widowed daughter-in-law. The daughter-in-law becomes pregnant by the patriarch, and the patriarch, whose descendants will be the royal line of Israel—and eventually will include Jesus Himself—declares his deceiving daughter-in-law to be "more righteous" than himself. As the young people would say, "Ew-w-w!" More than a few sober saints wonder out loud what such an episode is doing in Scripture.

And it's not just discomfort with the content. The episode's placement, right in the middle of the story of Joseph, seems so out of place. Old Testament scholar E. A. Speiser, in his fine *Genesis* volume in the Anchor Bible series, describes this episode as "a completely independent unit," having "no connection with the drama of Joseph, which it interrupts at the conclusion of Act I."[3]

But there it is. Right there in Genesis. The story is not an oversight. The inspired author of Genesis thought it important enough to be relayed, in detail. Matthew highlighted it in his Gospel. These authors included it because they deemed it important, something not to be ignored; and yet we do. The more I study biblical narrative, the more impressed I am with both the marvelous artistry and meticulous craftsmanship of the biblical writers. And if we believe the Bible to be inspired, as I do, then we must accept that the authors—both human and divine—knew what they were doing.

Two inspired authors thought this story mattered, so it's up to us as earnest Bible students to see if we can understand why. But a mere recitation of the events, as I did above, leaves out precisely the factors most important in our effort to come to grips with this passage—the way in which the author tells the story.

The Bible writers' economy with words and skill in their portrayals of important events and characters means that their stories merit our full attention to how the author crafted his account. The story of Tamar begins this way: "At that time, Judah left his brothers" (Genesis 38:1).

The story begins with an explicit reference, "At that time," which refers us back to the end of the previous episode, in which Joseph had been sold by his brothers into slavery. The Tamar episode takes place immediately after the selling of Joseph and the convincing of Jacob that his son had died.

From Genesis to Revelation, biblical authors love to allude to God's previous saving actions, to compare and contrast characters, and to remind us subtly of previous episodes. "At that time" directs our attention to the previous episode, so that when we see the words "Judah left his brothers," we will be reminded that in the previous episode Joseph—at Judah's urging—had been sold away, and, as a result, Judah *left his brothers*.

If you think this makes too much of three words, consider this: the author had no need to mention that Judah left his brothers at all. He could have simply told us that Judah traveled to another place, or that he left to find a wife, or simply that he found a wife. But the author mentions that Judah "left his brothers," and at "that time," no less. What was Judah going to do, take ten brothers with him hunting for a bride? Not likely. Given the care with which the biblical stories are crafted, the words "left his brothers" are included because they indicate something significant. In this case, the words signify the parallel between Joseph leaving his brothers and Judah leaving his brothers. This alerts us to compare and contrast what each of these brothers did while separated from the rest.

After this opening, in five terse verses Judah marries; his (unnamed) wife gives birth to three sons, named Er, Onan, and Shelah, respectively; and enough time passes for an adult Er to marry Tamar. "But Er, Judah's firstborn, was wicked in the Lord's sight; so the Lord put him to death" (verse 7).

That's a devastating biography, and it's all we know of Er. Custom required that the deceased Er's next-of-kin marry Tamar, in order to give her a son—sorry, but in that culture, daughters don't count—to carry on the name of the dead husband. Judah complies.

"Then Judah said to Onan, 'Sleep with your brother's wife and fulfill your duty to her as a brother-in-law to raise up offspring for your brother.' But Onan knew that the child would not be his; so whenever he slept with his brother's wife, he spilled his semen on the ground to keep from providing offspring for his brother" (verses 8, 9).

With his elder brother, Er, dead, Onan takes the place of the firstborn. That means he will receive a double portion of his father's possessions when Judah dies. But if Onan gives a son to Tamar, *that* child—as heir of the firstborn—would inherit the double portion, not Onan. Duty or not, it is not to his material advantage to give Tamar a child, which explains his actions. Denying her in such a blatant fashion humiliates Tamar, and it reveals Onan to be cruel and greedy. No wonder that "what he did was wicked in the Lord's sight; so the Lord put him to death also" (verse 10). This is only a slightly longer biography for Onan than Er received, and more disgraceful.

Judah apparently does not know the particulars. From his perspective, he has given two sons to be Tamar's husband, and both have died. Note the irony here. In the previous episode, Judah and his brothers led Jacob to believe he had lost a son. In this episode, the evil behavior of Judah's offspring has cost him two sons. Only one son remains, putting Judah's legacy in jeopardy.

If Shelah should die, Judah would be left without heirs. Alarmed at this possibility, he makes an excuse, that his third son is too young to marry, and tells Tamar to go back and live with her father. No doubt she views this as a particular rejection. Though she is twice widowed, Judah neither provides for her a husband nor releases her to marry again. He sends her back to her father's household as a dependent rather than helping her become mistress of her own home.

And here we encounter a fascinating feature of biblical stories, something scholars call *type-scenes*, which we can think of as *story frameworks*. Every culture and literature has these. For example, in westerns it might be that a new sheriff comes to town. We can construct a whole plot based on that. In romantic comedies we have the classic "boy meets girl, boy loses girl, boy wins girl back," and they live happily ever after. The stories built on these basic frameworks can vary a great deal, and our enjoyment and appreciation of them grows as we discover how the characters and plot developments meet or contradict our expectations.

The Bible has at least half a dozen of these type-scenes, but at this point in the story of Tamar we begin to recognize a familiar one.

The Barren Woman

The "barren woman" story framework has already appeared prominently in the book of Genesis. First we have Sarah, the wife of Abram, who is advanced in years and has no children, but who then miraculously conceives a son, through whom the promise to Abram will be fulfilled. Rebecca has a similar situation. She and Isaac are married for twenty years before she conceives, and then she is blessed with twins. Her son Jacob will eventually give his new name, Israel, to God's chosen people. Jacob's wife, Rachel, remains childless for many years, making it the third generation in a row in which the wives of the patriarchs have had fertility problems. Rachel does eventually conceive and gives birth to two sons, one of them Joseph, who will deliver Israel from famine.

By this time, Judah's aunt, grandmother, and great-grandmother all had been a central character in a Barren Woman story, and each had given birth to a son who became an instrument of God's saving actions. That brings us to Judah, whose only daughter-in-law, Tamar, is childless.

The ancient listener, hearing this story for the first time, recognizes the significance of the Barren Woman framework and is alerted to look for comparisons and contrasts. A major contrast to the previous examples can be seen in Tamar, who is not barren because of her own infertility but because the men in her life have failed or denied her. Differences like this keep the story familiar and yet fresh and interesting—and they also hint at the eventual outcomes. This difference in the locus of infertility tells us to take note: reversal will be a major theme of the story.

With that in mind, at this point several questions arise: Will God enable Tamar somehow to give birth to a significant son? How will this be accomplished or thwarted? What will be the significance of that child, if she has one?

"After a long time Judah's wife, the daughter of Shua, died. When Judah had recovered from his grief, he went up to Timnah, to the men who were shearing his sheep, and his friend Hirah the Adullamite went with him" (verse 12).

This verse reveals a great deal to the ancient audience. Enough time has passed for Judah's wife to die, and for his time of grieving to pass. Judah has been a widower for some time. And it mentions that he is going up to Timnah, where his sheep were being sheared.

Shearing of sheep is an ancient special trade, going back at least two thousand years before Christ. Sheep shearing was the first big event after the passing of winter. To this day, those who keep sheep prefer to have them sheared early, before lambing time. Thus it was in Judah's day.

At the location where the shearing took place, there would be wool buyers and other merchants. The owners of the flocks could sell their wool and buy needed goods from other merchants. It was a general time of feasting and celebration. So, for Judah, we have the end of a long winter, both in terms of weather and, emotionally, the end of a period of grieving. He will be prepared to sell the wool and celebrate.

The slighted Tamar hears that Judah will go to shearing and formulates her strategy: "When Tamar was told, 'Your father-in-law is on his way to Timnah to shear his sheep,' she took off her widow's clothes, covered herself with a veil to disguise herself, and then sat down at the entrance to Enaim, which is on the road to Timnah. For she saw that, though Shelah had now grown up, she had not been given to him as his wife" (verses 13, 14).

The narrator wants us to know that, despite all the time that has passed, Tamar has remained faithful to both her deceased and potential future husbands. She still wears "widow's clothes," even though "a long time" had passed.

The narrator could have said that "Judah was on his way," but he uses the term "father-in-law," to emphasize the relationship between the two. Upon hearing that Judah is headed to the sheep shearers, and realizing that his wife has died, Tamar resolves to act. After removing her widow's clothes, she disguises herself with a veil and stations herself at a strategic point along the road from Judah's home to the sheep shearers at Timnah. And we are told specifically that she did this because she realized that Judah's third son had grown up but had not been given to her as her husband, as Judah had implied that he would do.

It has become clear to Tamar that Judah is not going to risk his third son, that no matter what he said before, he has effectively abandoned her. She also knows that as a widower he could remarry without dishonor because his grieving time had come to an end. He will have no more sons, at least not by his first wife. In addition, she knows that since he's going to the sheep shearing, he will anticipate receiving some money and may well be in the mood to celebrate.

She also reasoned that, with his wife having been dead for some time and Judah being a man of normal male appetites, he would be open to seeking physical gratification. But she positions herself on the road *to* Timnah. Apparently, she intends to encounter him *before* he has sold his wool, *before* he has collected the money. In fact, this is the key to her whole plan.

She needs to intercept Judah *before* he reaches Timnah because once he has sold the wool from his sheep, he will have abundant money to spend—*but she does not want money*. She wants justice; she wants what is owed her. She wants a son and legitimacy for that son as an heir to Judah. To succeed in that, she must intercept Judah and carry out her plan *before* he has money. Since he will not give her a husband to impregnate her, she will trick him into doing it himself, and do it in such a way that he cannot deny paternity. If he pays her and goes on his way, *she will fail.* Only if he leaves something identifiable with her can her plan succeed.

She stations herself near Enaim, disguised as a prostitute. The ambush is laid. The trap is set. Now she waits.

Sure enough, Judah encounters the disguised Tamar on his way to Timnah. Apparently it was the custom for prostitutes to veil their faces in public, so when Judah sees her veiled countenance, *he recognizes her profession* but *fails to identify her*—yet another layer of irony in a deeply ironic story. Judah approaches her and declares his desire for her services. Playing her part flawlessly, Tamar begins to haggle with him.

" 'And what will you give me to sleep with you?' she asked. 'I'll send you a young goat from my flock,' he said" (verses 16, 17).

After shearing he will have ready-money. A few weeks after that, the lambs and kids will be born, but on the day they meet, he has neither. He promises to send her a goat kid from his flock. In a culture where wealth is measured in livestock, it is a healthy fee. Yet he offers only a promise that he will do something in the future. Any real prostitute would refuse to accept a promise for future payment from someone she might never see again. This causes her to ask for a guarantee. " 'Will you give me something as a pledge until you send it?' she asked. He said, 'What pledge should I give you?'

" 'Your seal and its cord, and the staff in your hand,' she answered" (verses 17, 18).

Savvy woman Tamar asks for the equivalent of his driver's license and credit card. The objects were linked to his identity, and that is what she needs. Apparently eager for her favors, he agrees.

"So he gave them to her and slept with her, and she became pregnant by him. After she left, she took off her veil and put on her widow's clothes again" (verses 18, 19).

Ever economical, the biblical author provides everything we need to know in very few words. Tamar's veil, disguising her as a prostitute, is just that, a disguise. Having achieved her goal, she takes off her veil, puts on her widow's clothes again, and returns home. By doing this, she eliminates any questions regarding her real motives, and the child's paternity.

Her only "customer" had been Judah. Only Judah encountered her disguised as a prostitute, and immediately after he left she returned to her modest widow's attire. Only Judah could have impregnated her. Lest there be the slightest doubt, we are treated to this informative episode:

> Meanwhile Judah sent the young goat by his friend the Adullamite in order to get his pledge back from the woman, but he did not find her. He asked the men who lived there, "Where is the shrine prostitute who was beside the road at Enaim?"
>
> "There hasn't been any shrine prostitute here," they said.
>
> So he went back to Judah and said, "I didn't find her. Besides, the men who lived there said, 'There hasn't been any shrine prostitute here'" (verses 20–22).

By now you're beginning to understand how the biblical authors make their points. We have not only the author's account of her actions, we also have the testimony of the men of Enaim. To erase all doubts, the author records that the men of Enaim tell Adullam, "There hasn't been any shrine prostitute here," and then Adullam repeats it to Judah verbatim: *There hasn't been any shrine prostitute here.* The repetition makes the point emphatic: no one saw Tamar-as-prostitute—*except Judah*. If she's pregnant, only Judah can be the father. Why such emphasis? Because in this case, *establishing paternity beyond doubt is a life-and-death matter.*

"About three months later Judah was told, 'Your daughter-in-law Tamar is guilty of prostitution, and as a result she is now pregnant.' Judah said, 'Bring her out and have her burned to death!'" (verse 24).

Deep, deep irony here. Judah had patronized a prostitute whom no one else had seen, with whom he had left his signet and staff, and who could not be found in order to redeem his belongings. Now he is informed that Tamar must have been a prostitute, but he is blind to any potential connection between the two pieces of information. No doubt he is actually relieved by all this. If she is indeed guilty, this eliminates a problem for him. He doesn't have to risk losing his third and final son by giving him to Tamar as a husband. She will be eliminated from making any further claims on him, and she won't be sitting in her father's home, a living reminder of Judah's neglect of his obligation. Rather too eagerly, Judah sentences her to a painful death.

Now we see that the pledge she asked for is her only means of survival. She can escape death only if she is able to prove that Judah is the father of the child she carries.

"As she was being brought out, she sent a message to her father-in-law. 'I am pregnant by the man who owns these,' she said. And she added, 'See if you recognize whose seal and cord and staff these are.' Judah recognized them and said, 'She is more righteous than I, since I wouldn't give her to my son Shelah.' And he did not sleep with her again" (verses 25, 26).

We hear another echo of the previous episode when Tamar asks Judah to identify the seal and cord and staff. After selling Joseph into slavery, the brothers dipped his coat-of-many-colors into goat's blood, and then, rather than declaring Joseph dead, they asked Jacob to identify the robe. In this story, Judah is asked to identify his belongings left as a pledge for a goat.

Whatever else we may think of all this, Judah recognizes that Tamar had merely collected a debt, a legitimate debt—albeit in a very unorthodox fashion.

Of course, this whole episode is terribly troubling to a modern audience. We view this through the morals of our own time and place, and our sensibilities rebel against the notion of a daughter-in-law pretending to be a prostitute in order to seduce her father-in-law, or for the respected patriarch to be patronizing a prostitute and paying for sex at all! But those are our problems. The matter of an incestuous relationship remains, but we will deal with that later. Clearly, the narrator is not concerned with this, and moreover, he does not expect his audience to be put off either.

They will see this much more as a simple issue of justice: in a culture where a woman's security, especially in old age, is a husband or a son to care for her, this poor woman has no husband, even though her father-in-law is obligated and has promised to provide one. He has not been faithful to his responsibility to her, and she is not going into spinsterhood and poverty quietly.

The real question for us, however, is not whether we approve of Tamar's actions, or even whether Judah approved. After all, Judah's judgment in this whole episode has been sorely lacking. And remember, the narrator placed this whole episode in the middle of another, larger story, and explicitly invited us to compare and contrast Judah's actions—and Tamar's—with those of Joseph. What we need to understand is God's verdict on all this.

It is generally a mistake to judge actions in the distant past using the standards of today. If God approved of what was done, it is hazardous for us to find fault. And yet it happens all the time. Looking at an episode in the Old Testament, people often declare, "I can't believe in a God who . . . tolerated slavery, allowed women to be treated in such a way, called for the extermination of the Canaanites . . . [fill in your own pet peeve]." And yet, if the Bible is true, there is no Other. To condemn God is to take His place. Our task is to try to understand God's actions, not to judge them.

To do that, we will have to examine this entire episode—which has not quite finished—in relation to the larger context, which is where we turn next.

Judah declared Tamar "more righteous than I," but, given his conduct through this whole episode, that is faint praise. What was God's verdict? Often in biblical narratives, especially this early in the Bible, God's verdict is enacted rather than announced. And that's what we see here.

Tamar, impregnated in that single encounter, gives birth to twin boys. She receives the ultimate award: two sons to care for her, and through her the royal—and Messianic—line will pass. It's difficult to imagine what more she could have wished for, especially when we consider the special circumstances surrounding the birth of Tamar's twins. Of the first four generations of Abraham's line, two women have twins: Rebekah and Tamar. And in each case, there is something unusual about the birth of the twins. Tamar is being likened to Rebekah.

Then there's the whole question of why this story, this strange story, of Judah and Tamar has been placed in the middle of the dramatic and strategic Joseph narrative. As we saw earlier, Judah's behavior is being compared to Joseph's—that's why this episode fits here, between Joseph sold into slavery and Joseph's encounter with Potiphar's wife.

As mentioned earlier, Judah "left his brothers" after he was directly responsible for Joseph leaving his brothers through slavery. The brothers used the blood of a goat to persuade Jacob that Joseph had died. Tamar uses the signet and staff given in place of a goat to persuade Judah that he is the father of her twins. Judah, when he encounters someone he believes to be a prostitute, indulges the flesh. Joseph, when presented with the opportunity to indulge the flesh by Potiphar's wife, refuses.

Considering Judah alone, one would conclude that this is an episode in a series of episodes depicting the moral education and growth of Judah. He goes from being one who let his brother Joseph be sold into slavery to the one who offers to go to prison in order that his brother Benjamin might remain free. It is a long and arduous journey, but eventually Judah emerges as a worthy patriarch of the royal line. Even in the sorry episode of Tamar, he confesses his guilt. It is a step forward, after all.

But this story is not about Judah alone. Indeed, he is not the central character. He is not the one who drives the action, who determines the outcome. That honor belongs to the clever and resourceful Tamar.

Whatever we think of her approach, it is difficult to conceive of an alternative that would achieve justice. God would never coerce Judah into action. Judah refused to give Tamar another son as her husband. He would not have voluntarily impregnated his own daughter-in-law. We know this because after she revealed his paternity we are told, "He did not sleep with her again."

In fact, in a marvelous irony, she had bested men at their own game. As Lindsay Hardin Freeman remarked, "When Judah refused to give her his third son, as mandated by Jewish law, she seduced him to get her due: a child of her own. Throughout the Old Testament, men most often saw women as vessels to bear children. Here that order is reversed: Tamar uses Judah as a family vessel to deliver sperm."[4]

How does Tamar compare with famous men in the Bible? What male character displays Tamar's level of wisdom, cleverness, and resourcefulness? Who is her strong partner, her match?

Certainly not Judah. He does not fare well. Judah will be the progenitor of the eventual royal line, but this episode dramatically demonstrates that he is not ready for such responsibility or such honor. This is one installment in a series that ends with Judah willing to sacrifice his own freedom for his brother, but he is not that man here.

By contrast, Tamar's shrewd action and initiative portray one who possesses the wisdom needed to be a just ruler. She may be multiple generations previous to wise Solomon, but the inspired author's account of her ingenious solution to her predicament brings to mind an eerily parallel event early in that king's reign.

In 1 Kings 3, Solomon confronts the problem of two prostitutes, both claiming maternity of a single child. Only the two women know for certain whose child it is. One of them is lying, but which one? By his ingenious and famous dictum to cut the child in half, Solomon determines maternity by discovering which woman really has maternal feelings for the child.

This story occurs in 1 Kings as a testament to Solomon's wisdom. "When all Israel heard the verdict the king had given, they held the king in awe, because they saw that he had wisdom from God to administer justice" (1 Kings 3:28).

In the encounter of Judah and Tamar, she masquerades as a prostitute. Only the two of them know what happened, and Judah could not—did not—identify his sexual partner. Except for Tamar's insistence that Judah leave identifying possessions with her, he could have denied paternity; indeed, every part of this intricate plan has to work, or Tamar may lose her life. She must prove his paternity, even though he is unaware of it!

Tamar's task is far more difficult than Solomon's. And the stakes in this case are far higher. If Solomon is mistaken, the wrong woman gets the child. If Tamar does not succeed, she and her child will die!

You might object that Solomon didn't pretend to be a prostitute. No, but he either pretended to want to slice a baby in half—or he actually meant to do it! It's difficult to see how feigning murder is morally superior to feigning prostitution. You might object that Solomon didn't engage in sexual immorality. By our standards he did, since he had seven hundred wives and three hundred concubines. By the standards of his time, he did not. And, as Judah acknowledged, by the standard of his time, neither did Tamar.

Given the interesting parallels in the two stories—two prostitutes versus one pretended prostitute; disputed maternity versus unknown paternity; and the protagonist successfully establishing parenthood in both cases—they certainly appear similar. But given the greater difficulty and higher stakes in Tamar's case, it would be unfair to call her "the female Solomon."

Indeed, there is every reason to turn it around. Tamar is Solomon's ancestor, and she faces—and resolves—a more difficult and more urgent problem than Solomon does. In every point, the comparison favors Tamar. Yes, Solomon prayed for wisdom. But at least part of the answer to that prayer may have come in his DNA. He appears to have been born in the deep end of the gene pool, inheriting a shrewd and logical mind from his truly great grandmother—great nine times over. Of course, Tamar's shrewdness and her two sons were God's gift to her. So, rather than ranking them, let us just say they are a match.

Earlier we talked about what scholars call *type-scenes*, which I have dubbed story frameworks. We have already seen how Tamar's tale fits into the Barren Woman framework. But with the conclusion of the story, discovering that the royal and Messianic lines both pass through her, we realize that the woman humiliated by her second husband and relegated to spinsterhood by her father-in-law also portrays the "rejected cornerstone."

You probably know the story. When Solomon built the temple, he had all the stones cut and dressed at the quarry, to maintain quiet at the building site. One stone didn't seem to fit anywhere, so the builders set it aside. Some even say they rolled it into a nearby valley to get it out of the way. But when it came time to set the cornerstone, the most important stone, it turned out to be the one they had rejected. The psalmist memorialized it thus: "The stone the builders rejected has become the cornerstone" (Psalm 118:22).

This is a story framework beloved by many cultures. Indeed, we have multiple manifestations of this in Western culture. Hans Christian Anderson's *Ugly Duckling* fits this framework. The bird condemned as ugly grows up to be an elegant swan. Even *Rudolph, the Red-nosed Reindeer* fits into this framework. The reindeer ridiculed for his appearance becomes the one who "saves Christmas."

Tamar, too, is rejected. She is not just barren—or, more accurately, not even barren. Her lack of children is not due to her infertility, but to her rejection by men unwilling to fulfill their responsibility to her. Onan pointedly spurns her, rejecting her as unworthy to carry his child. Judah then exiles her as essentially "bad luck." But in the end, she proves her worthiness by her wisdom and resourcefulness, risking everything on her wits. And God rewards her by granting her twins like Rebekah had, and by making her a progenitor of kings, and ultimately of the King of kings.

Why did God give such signal approval? I mean, prostitution, seduction, incest. Still, there's no getting around the fact that God approved of her actions. How can that be?

Again and again in Scripture, I find that God is amazingly practical. Yes, you read that correctly. *God is practical.* God recognizes that in a sinful world, sometimes we must choose the best available option among a group of less-than-ideal alternatives. Unable to achieve the ideal, we must settle for improvement, for *better*.

An example of God's practicality is the Bill of Divorcement. God instructed Moses that if a man divorced his wife, he must give her a Bill of Divorcement. But wait, doesn't Scripture say "God hates divorce"? Yes, He does. But there are things He hates even more—like forcing an honest woman to choose between prostitution and starvation. As Jesus later made clear, *one man plus one woman equals one flesh* was always God's plan.

But sin had marred that plan so badly that even Jesus' disciples, on hearing that divorce was forbidden except for adultery, said, "If this is the situation between a husband and wife, it is better not to marry" (Matthew 19:10). If the disciples, who had walked with the Son of God daily, who had the entire Old Testament to read, could not make the mental and psychological leap, then the Israelites in Moses' day had no chance. They had spent centuries in slavery, surrounded by Egyptian gods and ideas, and they did not have the written word. God realized they could not go from throwing women's belongings out of their tents, divorcing them at a whim, to lifelong monogamy in a single giant step. So He commanded the Bill of Divorcement, providing the woman with proof of the cause for the separation. If she had not been unfaithful, she might then be eligible for remarriage. It was far from ideal, but it was a practical improvement for women. It was *better*.

It is in this light that we must evaluate Tamar's actions. What was she to do? She had done no wrong. Under the laws she had a claim on Judah that he was unwilling to pay. She did not force him to do anything at sword point. She did not attempt to take revenge. She did not lie to him. Had he not approached her, seeking her services, nothing would have happened. The ideal being unavailable to her, she devised a practical alternative. She did not ask for more children or for money. She claimed no more than was her due.

Yes, Tamar engaged in sexual intercourse with her father-in-law. But she did not tempt Judah into being unfaithful to his wife. The narrator carefully points out that Judah's wife had died, and even the period of grieving had passed. It is true that Leviticus 18 forbids sexual relations between father-in-law and daughter-in-law. But that commandment was still four centuries in the future. Some have argued that she disguised herself because, if Judah had known who she was, he would have refused to impregnate her. Probably so. But that had less to do with her being his daughter-in-law than with his belief that she was "bad luck." She deceived Judah, but he had denied her every other means of restitution for her loss. It was not an ideal solution, but Judah had denied her that. She deserved *better*. And that is what she achieved.

Until I undertook this study, I always glossed over the story of Tamar. I didn't know what to make of it, and I knew that it made me deeply uncomfortable. Tamar's story has helped me understand that many of the most important stories make us—make me—uncomfortable. But then, the Faithful and True Witness tells us that our level of comfort is our problem. If Judah had been willing to move beyond his personal comfort, there would have been no need for Tamar to do what she did.

While this story is one of several episodes that show the character development of Judah, of how he becomes a worthy father of the royal line, the story is primarily about Tamar; about how she, through her determination and wisdom, confronts Judah with his own cowardice and selfishness. The obligation to care for widows runs throughout the Bible. We would hope that Judah, a leader among the sons of Israel, would be motivated to care for any widow. Yet for "a long time" he refuses to honor his obligation to his own twice-widowed daughter-in-law. The fact that she has to resort to such unusual tactics to obtain justice condemns him, not her.

We're uncomfortable for the wrong reasons. We're uncomfortable because of *what she did* instead of *what he failed to do*—honor his obligation to her. He claims that the third son who should be her husband is "too young." We should be outraged that Judah would treat her so, and leave her in such a desperate strait that she is forced to use extreme measures—to appeal to his passion—to receive the care that he should have volunteered out of compassion, or at least out of duty.

The story of Tamar affirms that the statement, "Pure religion and undefiled before our God and Father is this: to visit the fatherless and widows in their affliction, and to keep oneself unstained by the world" (James 1:27, WEB) was just as true in Judah's time as it is today.

Tamar did not make the rules. Men had done so. And when men denied her justice, she did what she could within their rules to achieve a practical justice, as Judah admitted. In a final irony, Judah had hoped to secure his legacy through his third son, Shelah, by refusing to allow him to marry Tamar. But in the end, Judah's great legacy as progenitor of royalty came through Tamar and her son Perez. The woman whom the men had rejected becomes the cornerstone, the mother of Judah's legacy.

I believe this episode depicts Tamar as a woman of surpassing wisdom and faith. Yes, faith—because there's more than mere cleverness evident here. What are the chances that she would conceive from one sexual encounter? It took great wisdom on the part of Tamar to plan and carry out this whole enterprise; but it also took great faith on her part that God would reward her quest for justice. Only God could grant Tamar the gift of a child—much less twins—and being progenitor of the royal and Messianic lines. Matthew will not let us forget or overlook that truth. So, no matter how uncomfortable this episode may make us, we cannot deny that God honored Tamar's faith and her actions—in signal fashion. The story of Tamar demonstrated what a single clever, determined woman could do.

---

1. Genesis 38:25.
2. Genesis 38:26.
3. E. A. Speiser, *Genesis*, The Anchor Bible (New York, Doubleday, 1964), 299.
4. Lindsay Hardin Freeman, *Bible Women: All Their Words and Why They Matter* (Cincinnati: Forward Movement, 2015), Kindle location 1128.

THREE

Jochebed
Cleverly Compliant

After generations in slavery, it is difficult for enslaved people to imagine that they might be free to disobey even the most minor commands. In fact, for them to truly be free is almost beyond their imagining. This is the situation we find Israel in at the beginning of the book of Exodus. God will need a human leader to help His people rally from their hopelessness and move from the relative comfort of captivity to the risk and responsibility of freedom. He needs a special man for this purpose. And, as we shall often find in Scripture, when God needs a special man, He provides a special woman to prepare that man. Or, in this case, a whole team of women.

Robert Anthony has said, "When you blame others, you give up your power to change." Surely Jochebed had plenty of reason to blame others—her people had endured four centuries of slavery under the greatest empire the world then knew. The Israelites were segregated, only allowed to live in one small area of Egypt. But throughout this story, Jochebed refuses to retreat into blame and self-pity. Instead, she takes the initiative, she plans for the future, and she acts decisively.

What a contrast with Pharaoh, ruler of that great empire, served by tens of thousands, builder of great funerary accommodations for himself, who, encountering what he saw as a problem, decided to blame others. He blamed the Israelites. "The children of Israel were fruitful and increased abundantly, multiplied and grew exceedingly mighty; and the land was filled with them" (Exodus 1:3, NKJV).

A strange cycle had occurred in Egypt. Joseph was brought there as a slave; a slave who eventually saved his own family and the Egyptian people from death through famine, but at great cost. We forget that Joseph also enslaved the Egyptian people. The grain he had stored during the good years he sold to them during the lean years. But over the seven years the cost for that grain was dear.

First they used all their money. When that ran out, they exchanged their livestock—which they could not feed anyway—for grain so that they did not starve. And when they had no more livestock, they sold themselves to Pharaoh. In this way, the slave who became viceroy of Egypt enslaved all the Egyptian people. Eventually, Pharoah returned the favor—when he thought the Israelites grew too numerous, he enslaved them. When they continued to grow despite hard labor, he commanded genocide. Throughout history, the justification for genocide has remained the same. There are too many of *them*; *they* are the problem. Kill *them*.

Predators have always found killing babies more palatable than executing adults, and that's where Pharaoh focused his efforts at genocide.

He first approached the midwives. If they kill the boys in their cribs, time will take care of Pharaoh's declared problem. Eliminate all the boy babies, and eventually the race will die out. The women and girls will marry Egyptians, the names of the Israelites will be lost, and Israel will be no more. Pharaoh no doubt reckoned that because midwives were often widows or other unattached women, they would have no recourse but to obey.

"Then the king of Egypt spoke to the Hebrew midwives, of whom the name of the one was Shiphrah, and the name of the other Puah; and he said, 'When you do the duties of a midwife for the Hebrew women, and see them on the birthstools; if it is a son, then you shall kill him; but if it is a daughter, then she shall live' " (verses 15, 16, NKJV).

Note that the midwives are *named*. That's the author's way of telling us that these women are important. He could have just referred to them as midwives, but he tells us there are two, named Shiphrah and Puah. And the reason for their importance quickly becomes evident—they refuse to cooperate with Pharaoh's command.

"But the midwives feared God, and did not do as the king of Egypt commanded them, but saved the male children alive" (verse 17, NKJV).

When summoned to explain their failure to comply, they dissimulate. "The king of Egypt called for the midwives and said to them, 'Why have you done this thing, and have saved the male children alive?' And the midwives said to Pharaoh, 'Because the Hebrew women are not like the Egyptian women; for they are lively and give birth before the midwives come to them' " (verses 18, 19, NKJV).

In other words, "Don't ask us to do it, we get there too late."

Pharaoh accepted this explanation. It's surprising, but it shouldn't be. Speaking as a man, I can tell you, men are mystified by women. We are bewildered by women in general, but women's physiology, their bodily functions—menstruation and childbirth—these are baffling for most men. This male cluelessness regarding women shows up repeatedly in Scripture.

For example, there is the account of Laban catching up to an escaped Jacob and his clan at Mount Gilead. There Laban confronts Jacob concerning his missing household gods. Not knowing that Rachel has taken them, Jacob claims innocence and challenges Laban to search through his entire camp to find them, and that if they are found, whoever has taken them shall die.

Rachel, of course, knows that she stole them, and she knows that she has to act quickly or they will be found and her life will be forfeited. She places the items under a camel saddle in her tent and then sits on the saddle. When Laban comes to search her belongings, she remains seated, saying, "Don't let my lord be angry that I can't rise up before you; for I'm having my period" (Genesis 31:35, WEB).

She's counting on male squeamishness, and she is not disappointed. Laban retreats, as she knew he would, without going near the camel saddle.

Something like that is at work here. Pharaoh has no idea about childbirth, and no curiosity about it either. Pharaoh, the Lord of Lower and Upper Egypt, is not immune to male bafflement when it comes to female physiology. When the midwives tell him that the Hebrew women are all more vigorous and uniformly give birth rapidly, Pharaoh accepts it.

These mutinous midwives defy Pharaoh's authority, and they are rewarded by God explicitly for these actions. "God dealt well with the midwives, and the people multiplied, and grew very mighty. Because the midwives feared God, he gave them families" (Exodus 1:20, 21, WEB).

Note that we know the midwives' names but not those of their husbands. Thus the text implicitly recognizes them as the heads of their families. Israel may not have been ready for this. Probably its culture could not adjust to such a thought. Yet, as the inspired author tells us, God gave families to the midwives, and we know the families only by the names of Shiphrah and Puah.

Rabbinic tradition holds that Shiphrah and Puah were mother and daughter, and that this mother and daughter were in fact Jochebed and Miriam! If that is true, then the next verses serve as confirmation that God honored His promise to the midwives, as it shows Shiphrah/Jochebed getting married and bearing a child. Certainly the spirit of the midwives in this episode will be echoed by Jochebed and Miriam as they conspire to save Moses from Pharaoh's death decree.

Frustrated by the midwives' failure, Pharaoh next commands that all the boy babies be thrown in the Nile. And with that, the first chapter of Exodus ends.

At this point Jochebed enters the narrative. Amram marries her, and the narrator is careful to point out that both he and Jochebed are members of the Levite tribe. With the entry of Jochebed, the action moves from the passive resistance of the midwives not acting to active resistance by Jochebed. She hides her boy child for three months. But that soon becomes impractical. Pharaoh has decreed that her son be cast into the Nile, and Jochebed decides to comply.

"When she could no longer hide him, she took a papyrus basket for him, and coated it with tar and with pitch" (Exodus 2:3, WEB).

The Hebrew word here translated "basket" is *tevah*. This is the only use of the word in the Old Testament other than in the Genesis story of the Flood, where it is rendered "ark." In case we miss this allusion to Noah's ark, the author mentions that she waterproofed this "ark" with "pitch," similar to the coating used by Noah. The author wants us to see Moses as a new Noah, who will, we can now expect, be delivered from death in the water by this boat, and the watch care of God.

"She put the child in it, and laid it in the reeds by the river's bank. His sister stood far off, to see what would be done to him" (verses 3, 4, WEB).

Here is another interesting irony. Pharaoh had commanded that Hebrew boys be cast into the river, and Jochebed can surely argue that she is obeying the command. After all, she is putting her son in the river. This is a wonderful example of how the letter of the law and the spirit of the law can be opposites. Pharaoh intends that the boy babies will drown or perhaps be eaten by crocodiles. By placing her child in this carefully constructed boat, and having his sister Miriam watch, Jochebed clearly hopes that the child will survive.

"Pharaoh's daughter came down to bathe at the river. Her maidens walked along by the riverside. She saw the basket among the reeds, and sent her servant to get it. She opened it, and saw the child, and behold, the baby cried. She had compassion on him, and said, 'This is one of the Hebrews' children' " (verses 5, 6, WEB).

"Pharaoh's daughter came down to bathe . . ." The biblical narrator, ever economical, does not tell us what Jochebed looked for when she placed the ark with Moses in it in the river, but the arrival of Pharaoh's daughter tells us a great deal. Surely Jochebed carefully selected the spot where she launched the papyrus ark with its precious cargo into the Nile. Perhaps it was a stretch of shoreline that crocodiles did not frequent, or perhaps they were kept clear of this area because Pharaoh's daughter frequently bathed there. Exactly how Jochebed knew of this—if she did—and how she selected the location, we do not know. We do know it produced the desired result, and then some.

The reaction of Pharaoh's daughter is fascinating. Perhaps out of curiosity, she asks her attendant to bring her the basket she sees floating in the reeds. She opens it and sees the baby, who promptly begins crying. And immediately she recognizes that it must be a Hebrew child, for the narrator has her declare that explicitly. "This is one of the Hebrews' children."

With her being Pharaoh's daughter, you would expect that she would share her father's concern about the multiplying of the Hebrews. If she does, there is no evidence of it here. Quite the contrary. The narrator leaves no doubt, by stating, "She had compassion on him."

"Then his sister said to Pharaoh's daughter, 'Should I go and call a nurse for you from the Hebrew women, that she may nurse the child for you?' Pharaoh's daughter said to her, 'Go.' The maiden went and called the child's mother. Pharaoh's daughter said to her, 'Take this child away, and nurse him for me, and I will give you your wages' " (verses 7–9, WEB).

This is really quite an extraordinary exchange. Miriam emerges from the reeds and has obviously overheard what Pharaohs' daughter said regarding the child, because she inquires as to whether she should find a nurse among the Hebrew women to serve as, essentially, a nanny.

Pharaoh's daughter has to realize what is happening here. She's clever enough to have identified the child as Hebrew, and it takes no great reasoning to conclude that the girl waiting nearby might well be his sister. And that the "Hebrew woman" she is going to choose as a nurse will in fact be the child's mother. Pharaoh's daughter reacts in an amazing fashion, telling Miriam to take the child with her to the nurse and that she, Pharaoh's daughter, will pay wages for the service.

Don't forget, Jochebed is a slave. Pharaoh's daughter *owns* her. She need only command the woman to do her bidding and Jochebed would be bound—and no doubt happy—to do it. In addition, Pharaoh's daughter very likely realizes that the nurse will be in fact the child's mother. This brings about an extraordinary circumstance in which Pharaoh's daughter will pay a Hebrew slave woman to take care of her own son—a son whom both of them were legally bound to drown in the river. We can almost see the winks and nods as these women enter into what can only be described as a conspiracy to circumvent Pharaoh's will. But of course there are no winks or nods, as the neutral narration indicates. These women are far too wise to give even the slightest indication that they are maneuvering around the express will of the dominant man.

"The woman took the child, and nursed it. The child grew, and she brought him to Pharaoh's daughter, and he became her son. She named him Moses, and said, 'Because I drew him out of the water' " (verses 9, 10, WEB).

So far, we have had four named women involved in the efforts to preserve Moses. The two midwives, Shiphrah and Puah, his mother Jochebed, and his sister Miriam. Pharaoh's daughter makes number five. And yet the team of women is not yet complete.

Moses, returned to Pharaoh's household as a youth, retained his identity as a Hebrew. Years later, when he saw an Egyptian mistreating a Hebrew, Moses killed the Egyptian and buried him in the sand. Sometime after, when he saw two Hebrews fighting, he admonished them. One of them challenged Moses by inquiring who put him in charge of them and then asked, "What are you going to do? Kill me like you did the Egyptian?"

Realizing that his crime had become known, Moses fled for his life. "Moses fled from the face of Pharaoh, and lived in the land of Midian, and he sat down by a well" (verse 15, WEB).

This sitting down by a well strikes us as rather unremarkable, but not to the ancient reader of the books of Genesis and Exodus. For them, this simple statement is the equivalent of us watching a video clip of a man wearing a gun belt riding into a town in the Old West and tying his horse up at the saloon. Something significant is about to happen. How does the ancient reader know that?

We've already talked about two different type-scenes, or what I call story frameworks. We've looked at The Barren Woman, and The Rejected Cornerstone. What we have here is the beginning of a Betrothal Narrative. The Betrothal Narrative goes like this:

1. The protagonist, usually the prospective groom, goes to a foreign land. In this case, Moses has gone to Midian.
2. The prospective groom then goes to a well, which is precisely what Moses does here.
3. At this well, the prospective groom meets a girl or girls.
4. Next, someone offers to draw water and then does so.
5. The girl or girls then rush back home, telling their father about it.
6. The stranger is then invited to share a meal
7. After which, a betrothal takes place.[1]

By the time we get to Exodus 2, this type-scene has already played out at least twice. First, there was Eliezer, Isaac's servant, who went seeking a bride for Isaac. It is, as you have noticed, a variation on the scene, something very common. In that case, instead of the prospective groom, Isaac, going to the well, his surrogate Eliezer went to the well where he encountered Rebekah, who drew water for him and his camels. Rebekah then rushed back to her house to tell of Eliezer's offer. Eliezer was invited to a meal, after which the betrothal was announced, thus completing the Betrothal Narrative type-scene.

And then there is the situation with Jacob, who, like Moses, flees for his life to a foreign land. Upon reaching that foreign land he finds shepherds around a well. He announces that he is seeking his uncle Laban, and they inform him that they expect Laban's shepherd to arrive soon. Jacob looks up and sees Rachel, with whom he is instantly enchanted. Then, in an impressive show of strength, he singlehandedly removes the stone covering on the well to allow the shepherds to draw water. Rachel rushes back home to tell her father, Laban, of her encounter. Laban then invites Jacob to dinner. A betrothal follows quickly.

So when Moses sits down by a well in this foreign land, the reader waits with anticipation—and we are not disappointed.

"Now the priest of Midian had seven daughters. They came and drew water, and filled the troughs to water their father's flock. The shepherds came and drove them away; but Moses stood up and helped them, and watered their flock. When they came to Reuel, their father, he said, 'How is it that you have returned so early today?' They said, 'An Egyptian delivered us out of the hand of the shepherds, and moreover he drew water for us, and watered the flock.' He said to his daughters, 'Where is he? Why is it that you have left the man? Call him, that he may eat bread' " (verses 16–20, WEB).

Notice how closely this episode follows the formula of the Betrothal Narrative. The only significant variation here is that instead of one girl, there are seven daughters.

Oh, yes, and the final part?

"Moses was content to dwell with the man. He gave Moses, Zipporah, his daughter" (verse 21, WEB).

Compared to the other instances of the Betrothal Narrative, this may seem too simple, too elementary to count. But as Robert Alter points out:

> These few verses may seem so spare a treatment of the convention as to be almost nondescript, but in fact this is just the kind of betrothal type-scene needed for Moses. To begin with, any presentation that would give more weight to Zipporah than merely one nubile daughter out of seven would throw the episode off balance, for her independent character and her relationship with Moses will play no significant role in the subsequent narrative.[2]

In other words, the way the author handles this convention, this type-scene, foreshadows the significance of Moses' wife and the rest of his story. She appears only once later in the story of Moses, and that is in a very strange scene. The author hints at her limited role by giving her scant mention, even in her own Betrothal Narrative.

Like the other type-scenes, you want to keep the Betrothal Narrative in the back of your mind. We will encounter it again.

By now, we have come to realize that the inspired authors are meticulous in their composition. Nothing is included in these narratives by accident. Names and numbers and incidents are included only if they matter. The daughters of Jethro, then, present us with a puzzle. Why tell us there were seven of them and only name one of them?

You may say, "Well, the other six don't matter." If that is so, why mention them at all? The narrative would be just as accurate if it said that Moses met Zipporah at the well. Yes, the others were were there, but they play no further role in the narrative, and if they play no further role, there is no need to mention them. But the inspired author clearly thinks we need to know that there were seven of them. Apparently, the number itself matters. Why?

If you recall, before these seven daughters, there were five significant women mentioned in the narrative of Moses: Shiphrah and Puah, the midwives; Jochebed, Moses' mother; Miriam, his sister; and Pharaoh's daughter. If you add in these seven daughters of Jethro, you come to a grand total of twelve. Again, the wit and wisdom of Leslie Hardin Freeman gives us the following insight: "Twelve women in a row protect Moses and help his journey through birth, life, boyhood, and young adulthood in just the first two chapters of Exodus. What? Twelve tribes of Israel, twelve apostles of Jesus . . . yet this all-female cast of twelve is often overlooked. Shocking."[3]

She is right to note that this group of twelve females is often overlooked, but that is not the fault of the biblical authors. As has happened often in this study, I was chagrined to realize that I had missed this telling detail previously, because I was not looking for it. Because I focused on Moses, I gave scant notice to the importance of Jochebed and almost entirely missed the crucial role the other women played. But there it is. Twelve women prepare Moses, who will lead the twelve tribes out of Egypt. The destiny of the twelve tribes depends upon the actions of these twelve women, of whom Jochebed is chief.

And that leads us to the answer of the final question: As a spiritual figure, whom does Jochebed match? We saw the parallels between Tamar and Solomon and declared them a match. Whose actions parallel those of Jochebed?

We've already mentioned that to some degree, her construction of the ark for Moses matches the actions of Noah. Just as Noah's ark—under God's watch care—delivered Noah and his family from the Flood, this ark delivers Moses from peril in the water. But Jochebed did much more than merely deliver Moses. She cared for him, nurtured him, and prepared him for life. Exactly how long Jochebed nursed Moses, we do not know. But we know that he was forty years old when he fled Egypt for Midian, that he spent forty years in Midian, and that he spent the last forty years of his life guiding Israel to the verge of the Promised Land.

The Bible says that God spoke to Moses face to face, as a man speaks to his friend. What an amazing statement! And when we look at the life of Moses, the one chosen to deliver Israel, we must remember the remarkable women involved in saving him—in delivering the deliverer. Without Jochebed, there is no Moses. Without Miriam to watch over him, there is no Moses. Without Pharaoh's daughter, who knowingly defies her father's command and saves the Hebrew child, there is no Moses. Moses will deliver the children of Israel through the waters of the Red Sea. Moses is the Deliverer of Israel; Jochebed is the main figure among those who deliver Moses. And there we find the match for Jochebed and the other eleven women who helped and guided Moses. Moses himself!

The story of Moses' deliverance includes the deaths of countless Hebrew boys cast into the Nile. But those deaths will be avenged in a signal fashion. When Moses delivers Israel through the Red Sea, Pharaoh commands his army to pursue the escaping Israelites. When the army charges into the dry seabed, the water closes over them, and they drown. The Hebrew boys who were drowned at Pharaoh's command are now matched by Egyptian boys—Pharaoh's army—*drowned at Pharaoh's command.*

We have now finished our look at the first two examples of Bible women who seized the initiative, in both cases directly contrary to the wishes of men in authority. And we find that the narratives of Tamar and Jochebed parallel those of Solomon and Moses respectively. The culture they lived in might have discounted their importance, but it is increasingly clear that the biblical authors, and, more important, God, did not.

When I began this study, I realized that God had often heard the appeals of women. I did not realize the full significance that biblical writers ascribed to these two women who appeared, on the surface, to be fairly minor characters. Tamar seemed to be an interruption, a distraction from the story of Joseph. Jochebed appeared to be a footnote in the story of Moses. The story of Jochebed demonstrated to me the importance of what psychologists call a "support structure." Jochebed prepared the basket and put Moses in it. But she needed Miriam to watch it and, eventually, to intercede with Pharaoh's daughter. The Egyptian princess had the power to save the boy's life, but she needed Jochebed to prepare him for life. The midwives, Shiphrah and Puah, also had their roles to play. Raising up a hero like Moses in such a hostile environment required the assistance of several heroines, each of whom faced significant risks. These first two narratives have been filled with unexpected depth and beauty. What other surprises await us?

---

1. The Betrothal Narrative type-scene is discussed at length in Alter, *The Art of Biblical Narrative*, 62.
2. Alter, *The Art of Biblical Narrative*, 68.
3. Freeman, *Bible Women*, 34.

FOUR

Rahab
Faithful Spy

While this *is* a story we tell to children, we tend to camouflage one salient fact: Rahab is a prostitute. We tell the children she was an innkeeper, and that is probably true in the sense that she had rooms where people slept. But no fewer than five places in Scripture identify her as a prostitute. That is almost certainly one reason that Matthew included Rahab in his genealogy. In our examination of women of initiative, Rahab is the third chronologically, and the second of the four included in Matthew's genealogy. The first, as you recall, was Tamar, who pretended to be a prostitute.

Because this is a story we tell to children, we are familiar with the broad outline of events. Joshua sends two spies to Jericho, where they enter the house of Rahab, a prostitute. Soldiers of Jericho come to Rahab's house, seeking the spies. She hides them on the roof under some bales of flax. And then she lies to the soldiers, stating that the spies have just left, and that the soldiers should hurry and pursue them. She then makes a deal with the two spies—she will help them escape, and they must promise her that when the Israelites come to seize Jericho, she and her father's household will be spared. The spies agree, directing her to place a scarlet cord in her window as an indicator that her house is to be protected. Then they escape.

As we have discovered, these Old Testament stories are carefully crafted, and much of the significance is encoded in the details. The first notable detail is the difference in the number of spies as compared with the previous episode forty years earlier, when twelve spies were sent into the land. Ten of them convinced the rest of Israel not to invade the Promised Land—that the inhabitants were too fearsome and too strong. Only two of those spies, Caleb and Joshua, gave a faithful report. They were faithful not only in reporting the actual conditions of the land but also were filled with faith that God would deliver it to them.

Forty years elapsed, during which time all of the Israelites older than twenty years of age perished in the desert—all except Caleb and Joshua. After Moses' death, Joshua succeeds him as leader. When Joshua sends two spies, this signals that they will be faithful—as Joshua and Caleb had been decades earlier. But, in contrast to the twelve spies sent forty years before, these two spies are not named. As we shall see, there's a very good reason for that. One reason is that the real players in this episode are not the two spies but the two characters named in the first verse of Joshua 2—Joshua and Rahab.

Rahab does almost all the talking in this episode. In fact, Lindsay Hardin Freeman, in her book *Bible Women: All Their Words and Why They Matter*, tells us that in the whole book of Joshua, women speak 277 words, and that Rahab speaks all but 22 of those, and most of those in a single speech. Given that the Bible is usually fairly sparse in the number of words that it allots a given character, Rahab's words must be significant.

In fact, Rahab utters most of these—172 words—right after she brings the spies down from the roof where she had hidden them, unburdening herself with this remarkable speech:

> She said to the men, "I know that Yahweh has given you the land, and that the fear of you has fallen upon us, and that all the inhabitants of the land melt away before you. For we have heard how Yahweh dried up the water of the Red Sea before you, when you came out of Egypt; and what you did to the two kings of the Amorites, who were beyond the Jordan, to Sihon and to Og, whom you utterly destroyed. As soon as we had heard it, our hearts melted, and there wasn't any more spirit in any man, because of you: for Yahweh your God, he is God in heaven above, and on earth beneath. Now therefore, please swear to me by Yahweh, since I have dealt kindly with you, that you also will deal kindly with my father's house, and give me a true sign; and that you will save alive my father, my mother, my brothers, and my sisters, and all that they have, and will deliver our lives from death" (Joshua 2:9–13, WEB).

The more you look at it, the more amazing the speech appears. She uses the metaphor of melting away to describe the way resistance to the Israelites has and will dissipate. In a way similar to some of the psalms, she recites the mighty deeds of Israel's God. She concludes her oration about Yahweh with an amazing prophetic speech and declaration of faith by stating that He is "God in heaven above, and on earth beneath." And then she extracts the promise of protection.

Having secured their promise to protect her—they have little choice, since she could still turn them in—she proceeds to demonstrate her cunning by instructing them on how to escape:

"Then she let them down by a cord through the window; for her house was on the side of the wall, and she lived on the wall. She said to them, 'Go to the mountain, lest the pursuers find you. Hide yourselves there three days, until the pursuers have returned. Afterward, you may go your way' " (verses 15, 16, WEB).

"The mountain" she referred to lies to the west of Jericho, while the Israelites are camped well to the east. She correctly discerns that those searching for the spies will go to the east, to catch spies they expect to be running home. The spies followed her sage advice.

"They went, and came to the mountain, and stayed there three days, until the pursuers had returned. The pursuers sought them all along the way, but didn't find them. Then the two men returned, descended from the mountain, crossed the river, and came to Joshua the son of Nun" (verses 22, 23, WEB).

The spies report to Joshua, essentially repeating verbatim what Rahab had said to them.

Rahab's first words to the spies	The spies' report to Joshua
"I know that *Yahweh has given you the land,* and that the fear of you has fallen upon us, and that *all the inhabitants of the land melt away before you.*"	They said to Joshua, "*Truly Yahweh has delivered all the land* into our hands. Moreover, *all the inhabitants of the land melt away before us.*"

In essence, Rahab *is* the spy. She harbors the two unnamed spies, gives them the equivalent of a military situation report, saves them from discovery, helps them get outside the city walls, and instructs them on how to elude their pursuers. When they get back to Joshua, they repeat her words almost verbatim. Everything Joshua instructed the spies to do, Rahab makes possible. Rahab collaborates with Joshua to accomplish his purpose. So, in a sense, they are a match. Perhaps this explains a rabbinic tradition that claims she married Joshua. But Matthew's genealogy declares she married Salmon, of the tribe of Judah.

In fact, there is a better spiritual match for Rahab: Caleb. Caleb and Joshua collaborated to be faithful spies, but *like* Rahab and *unlike* Joshua, Caleb was not an Israelite by birth. Caleb was a Kenizzite. And yet, because of his faithfulness, he was allotted an inheritance as an Israelite. Rahab, because of her faithfulness, becomes part of the royal and Messianic lines. Caleb demonstrated great courage, not only as a spy in his younger days but also forty-five years later:

I was forty years old when Moses the servant of Yahweh sent me from Kadesh Barnea to spy out the land. I brought him word again as it was in my heart. . . . Moses swore on that day, saying, "Surely the land where you walked shall be an inheritance to you and to your children forever, because you have wholly followed Yahweh my God."

. . . Now, behold, I am eighty-five years old, today. As yet I am as strong today as I was in the day that Moses sent me. . . . Now therefore give me this hill country, of which Yahweh spoke in that day; for you heard in that day how the Anakim were there, and great and fortified cities. It may be that Yahweh will be with me, and I shall drive them out, as Yahweh said (Joshua 14:7, 9–12, WEB).

At eighty-five years old, he's still ready to take on the walled cities! By contrast, Rahab was a woman; but she helped conquer the walled city of Jericho, and when unexpectedly confronted with the Hebrew spies and questioned by soldiers of the king of Jericho, she had the presence of mind and the courage to save the spies, and as a result she saved herself and all her father's household. But more than that, her breathtaking testimony of faith in Israel's God—worthy of a prophet—places her among the great figures of faith in all of Scripture.

We noted that Rahab and Joshua are the two characters named in Joshua 2. In fact, they are the *only* two characters named in the entire episode! The king of Jericho—an important person, surely—is not named; only these two faithful spies, Rahab and Joshua, are named. And when we look at it, what real spying is done? There is no information about troop numbers, armaments, or deployment; no information about the wall's weaknesses or blind spots. Only Rahab's testimony is shared, that the people are afraid because they know that Joshua's God is powerful! Rahab's behavior and faith do indeed match that of gallant Caleb: two faithful Gentiles who played essential roles in Israel's conquest of the Promised Land. And God recognized Rahab by causing the royal and Messianic lines to pass through her.

Tamar and Jochebed were both matriarchs—Tamar as the progenitor of kings, Jochebed as the mother of Israel's lawgiver and deliverer. Rahab is both matriarch of the royal line and prophet in her declaration of the greatness of Israel's God and the certainty of His victory. This study of her life revealed to me her intelligence and courage. Other character traits will become more evident as we encounter her son, who will appear as a significant character in the story of another of our heroines.

FIVE

DEBORAH
GENERAL AND JUDGE

In 1975, my wife and I moved to Waukegan, Illinois, on the shores of the inland freshwater sea called Lake Michigan. We often saw the great freighters and ore boats that plied the waters of the Great Lakes from Duluth on Lake Superior all the way to the Atlantic Ocean. In November of that year, on Lake Superior, a large ore boat went down with the loss of all twenty-nine hands. Stories consisting of a few terse paragraphs, with such headlines as "*Edmund Fitzgerald* reported missing," appeared in the back sections of newspapers in ports all along the Great Lakes. Still settling into a new home and new school year, I did not notice these at the time.

Then Gordon Lightfoot's song, "The Wreck of the *Edmund Fitzgerald*," was released. Its haunting melody and lyrics brought home many of the details of the story, and the emotional toll on the families, not only of those lost but of all those who sail these inland seas. It got my attention, stirred my emotions, and led me to look up the old newspaper accounts to try to better understand the tragedy.

Later, I realized that this is part of a much older tradition. As we shall see, it goes back at least to the time of Deborah in the Old Testament. Narrative accounts of various events are passed down. But to mark significant events—tragedies and triumphs—we often write songs. As another example, long before I knew the simple facts of the 1900 railroad disaster, I heard a song about Casey Jones, the locomotive engineer and hero who died in a train collision in order to save his passengers. And before I read the newspaper accounts of the sinking, I heard the song, "The Wreck of the *Edmund Fitzgerald*." The narrative stories give the facts; the songs convey the emotional impact. And that is what we have in the story of Deborah. Judges 4 provides the "newspaper account," terse and minimalist. Judges 5, the Song of Deborah and Barak, celebrates the victory and God's providence. Each account complements the other. Indeed, only by putting the two accounts together do we see the comprehensive picture of what happened.

We begin, as Scripture does, with the narrative account—the facts, ma'am, just the facts. "Again the Israelites did evil in the eyes of the Lord, now that Ehud was dead" (Judges 4:1).

These words describe an all-too-familiar pattern in Israelite history. God would raise up a righteous leader to rescue the people and restore their faith. And so long as that leader lived, the people respected his or her example and ordered their lives accordingly. God blessed their reformed behavior, and they prospered.

But in that age, as in any other, prolonged prosperity breeds unwarranted self-confidence in human beings. We come to believe that prosperity is the natural order of things and that we can indulge ourselves in activities that are less than productive. Such times are often followed by a time of trial.

Ehud had delivered them from the tyranny of Moab. But when Ehud died, they forgot that the reforms he fostered had brought them peace and prosperity. So God had to remind them. "The Lord sold them into the hands of Jabin king of Canaan, who reigned in Hazor. Sisera, the commander of his army, was based in Harosheth Haggoyim. Because he had nine hundred chariots fitted with iron and had cruelly oppressed the Israelites for twenty years, they cried to the Lord for help" (verses 2, 3).

Hazor, the city where Jabin king of Canaan reigned, lies within the territory given to the tribe of Naphtali. Their tribal lands ran from the western shore of the Sea of Galilee east to the foot of the region known today as the Golan Heights, on the southwestern border of modern-day Lebanon, and westward slightly more than half the way from the Jordan River to the Mediterranean Sea. It includes the city of Dan, the northernmost large city in Israel at the time. The expression "From Dan to Beersheba" encompasses the entire north-south length of Israel.

So Jabin and his army are an occupying force, displacing Israelites of the tribe of Naphtali, taking their land, occupying their homes, and committing all the other grim acts that occupation entails. Their homes, their crops, their wives and daughters, their children—nothing is safe; no one escapes the routine abuse.

And if you substitute the phrase "Abrams battle tanks" for "chariots fitted with iron," you get a sense of the military power the Israelites faced, and the threat they lived under for twenty years. As happens to all of us, in times of difficulty they realized their need for God's watch care.

"Now Deborah, a prophet, the wife of Lappidoth, was leading Israel at that time. She held court under the Palm of Deborah between Ramah and Bethel in the hill country of Ephraim, and the Israelites went up to her to have their disputes decided" (verses 4, 5).

In these few words, we get a picture of the tremendous power Deborah held. First, her designation as a prophet means that the people recognized that *she spoke for God*. We tend to think of prophesying as predicting the future, but throughout Scripture the main function of a prophet is to reveal God's will, counsel, and admonition to His people. She will make predictions in this episode, but that is not her primary function. Whether making predictions or not, she served to relay God's will to His people.

When we hear the word *judge*, we see a courtroom. To be a judge in Israel at this time meant to be a national leader, including in the military realm. Gideon and Samson, as two examples, were known almost exclusively for their military achievements. More to the point, as the story of Solomon tells us, judging in the sense of settling disputes was a function of a monarch. Deborah, then, is a leader in the broadest sense of that term, functioning as a monarch would, yet without the power of coercion. She has true power, the power of influence, the power of trust. The Israelites "went up to her to have their disputes decided" because they saw that she was a woman led by God, and they trusted her character and her wisdom.

So comprehensive had her influence become that the palm tree where she held court was simply referred to by her name, "Deborah's Palm," and Israelites journeyed there to have her hear their disputes. It gives you some idea of the tremendous stature she had. But we're about to see it become even bigger.

"She sent for Barak son of Abinoam from Kedesh in Naphtali and said to him, 'The Lord, the God of Israel, commands you: "Go, take with you ten thousand men of Naphtali and Zebulun and lead them up to Mount Tabor. I will lead Sisera, the commander of Jabin's army, with his chariots and his troops to the Kishon River and give him into your hands" ' " (verses 6, 7).

Deborah's palm tree stood between Ramah and Bethel, far to the south of Hazor and the Canaanite occupation. She lived in the tribal lands of Ephraim and Hazor, and as we mentioned, reigned in the lands of Naphtali. This explains why "she sent for Barak . . . from Kedesh in Naphtali." Deborah directs him to assemble an army of ten thousand men from Naphtali and Zebulun. The map makes it clear why. Naphtali and Zebulun are the areas oppressed by Jabin. His capital is located in tribal lands of Naphtali, and the major battle will be fought in the land of Zebulun.

From our perspective, it may seem curious that Deborah does not lead an army of Ephraimites—that is, an army of the people who live closest to her—or perhaps call for enlistments from all of Israel.

From the earliest days, getting Israelites to leave their homes and fight for land allotted to other tribes had been difficult. The song of Deborah and Barak in Judges 5 specifically mentions the tribes of Dan and Asher as two tribes that refuse to join. And although Judges 4 only mentions Naphtali and

Zebulun, chapter 5 says that the princes of Issachar were also with Deborah. Again a map makes clear why that is so. All the fighting described in the two chapters takes place in the contiguous land of those three tribes: Naphtali, Zebulun, and Issachar. The men of these three tribes will be defending their own homes, their own families.

Deborah lays out the plan of battle in advance. Barak will take his army to Mt. Tabor. Deborah says that God will draw Sisera and his ironclad chariots to the Kishon River. The arrival of the chariots will be Barak's signal to attack. Deborah assures him that the Lord will deliver the Canaanite army, including its chariots of iron, into his hand.

But Barak, whose name means "lightning," is ironically reluctant to strike. He tells Deborah that if she will not go with him, he will not go. If we had any lingering doubts about who the real leader is, this comment by Barak clears it up once and for all. He will not lead the army unless she consents to accompany him. She agrees to come but tells him that because of his reluctance, the honor for winning the battle will go to a woman. No doubt Barak thought the woman would be Deborah, and the reader is tempted to think that also. However, it turns out differently.

Exactly how Barak and the Israelites defeated the Canaanites is not specified in chapter 4, but chapter 5, verse 4 (WEB) gives us a hint: "The earth trembled, the sky also dropped. Yes, the clouds dropped water."

Jabin assembled his ironclad chariots in the river valley. Apparently, when the rainstorms came, the water drained into that valley, saturating the ground and turning it into a trap for Jabin's chariots. The weight of the iron on the narrow chariot wheels caused them to sink into the mire and become stuck, converting the ironclad chariots from an asset into a liability when Barak and his infantry attacked. The charioteers, armed for mobile fighting, not hand-to-hand combat, were ill-equipped to meet the Israelite foot soldiers. The initial attack would have rolled through the Canaanite ranks, its sheer momentum driving many Canaanites into the now flooding river. "The river Kishon swept them away, the age-old river, the river Kishon" (Judges 5:21).

Deprived of their mobile strike force, pressed against the river, unable to form an orderly retreat, the remaining Canaanite army would be forced to abandon the now worse-than-useless chariots and run for their lives. As is often the case, the fleeing army is at the mercy of its pursuers, and Judges tells us that "all Sisera's troops fell by the sword; not a man was left."

This probably does not mean that literally every man died, because as we shall soon see, Sisera survived and fled for his life. "Not a man was left" probably indicates that the Canaanite army suffered so many casualties that it became disorganized and ceased to exist as a fighting force. It was every man for himself, and the Israelite soldiers took down those trailing in the rear.

Despite this great victory on the battlefield, Deborah's prophecy about a woman receiving credit for the defeat of Sisera has yet to be fulfilled.

The general, we are told, fled on foot—another indication of the totality of defeat—until he came to the tent of Jael. She was the wife of Heber the Kenite. Scholars dispute the exact location of this encounter, but one suggestion is about halfway between Mt. Tabor and the Sea of Galilee. While we cannot be certain, this location makes sense, because it would indicate that Sisera was fleeing to Hazor.

In any case, he felt safe there, for the Canaanites were not at war with the Kenites, who were nomadic. Rather than go to war, these nomadic people would strike their tents and move on. So when Jael comes out of her tent and tells him to come in, that he need not fear anything, he believes her. Exhausted and dehydrated from his panicked retreat, he asks for water. Jael gives him milk. No doubt this comforts him, because she has gone beyond the minimum in supplying his needs. Considering what followed, it is possible she gave him warm milk as a sedative. In any case, with his stomach filled with milk, and his body exhausted from his flight, he falls into a sleep from which he will not awake.

A rabbinic tradition suggests that Sisera raped Jael, but the biblical text gives no support to this notion. However, her actions bespeak some deep anger on her part, for she kills him in an extremely violent and personal fashion. As he lies asleep, she takes a tent stake and a mallet, and drives the stake through his temple, out the other side, and into the ground. On the one hand, it sounds quite cold-blooded; on the other, it seems that some strong emotion must be driving that tent peg. And her seeming indifference to her deed when Barak arrives may indicate a suppressed rage.

Barak—once again, note the irony of "lightning's" tardy arrival—trailing Sisera, shows up at Jael's tent. There, the narrative portrays an eerily calm Jael.

"Just then Barak came by in pursuit of Sisera, and Jael went out to meet him. 'Come,' she said, 'I will show you the man you're looking for.' So he went in with her, and there lay Sisera with the tent peg through his temple—dead" (Judges 4:22).

Imagine yourself in Barak's place. After a long day of battle and pursuit, you see a nomad's tent. A woman comes out from it and tells you that she has the one you seek. She walks calmly toward her tent. You follow warily, sword drawn. But when you enter the tent you see the coagulating blood pooled under his head, and the tent peg protruding from his temple. You look at the woman with a new respect. That morning, Sisera was a fearsome figure, leader of an army, commander of three hundred chariots of iron. And now he lies dead in a nomad's tent, executed by this seemingly helpless woman.

At some point, it hit Barak that Deborah's prophecy had come true. Barak and his ten thousand men may have fought the battle, but Jael will be forever credited with the conquest of Sisera—an exalted warrior killed in his sleep by a lowly woman. But then, the so-called Song of Deborah and Barak is really the song of *three* women.

The more we examine it, the more remarkable the Song of Deborah and Barak becomes. The two male characters mentioned, Barak and Sisera, are clearly subordinate. Barak, the Israelite commander, refuses to attack without Deborah leading; Sisera, the Canaanite commander, falls by the hand of a solitary woman. The song takes a kind of morbid pleasure in dwelling on the scene of Sisera's mother gazing anxiously out the window, apprehensive that her son has taken so long to return. She comforts herself that he is busy plundering the Israelites, when in fact he is dead after fleeing the battle in disgrace.

Not only does this song give dramatic details of the battle, but it vividly describes Jael's assassination of Sisera in what seems lurid detail. As we find in several other episodes in the Old Testament, the song reveals a kind of savage joy that is unsettling to our ears. It should serve to remind us what courage these circumstances required from women such as Deborah and Jael. If this song celebrates the pain and helplessness of Sisera dying with a spike driven through his brain, imagine what frightful deeds the Canaanites would have sung about had the outcome been different. The joy with which this violence is related perhaps gives us an insight into the routine cruelty hidden in the terse phrase "cruelly oppressed," in Judges 4:2. The song is perhaps more understandable seen in the light of twenty years of Canaanite depredations.

There are a number of these victory songs in Scripture. We hear of the women singing of "Saul killing his thousands, and David his ten thousands"—much to the irritation of Saul, we might add. The other song of victory that comes to mind is the song of Moses after the victory of the Red Sea. In fact, the descriptions of the respective battles bear some similarities.

The biblical author could simply have said, "They sang praise to Yahweh for the victory he gave them," but he did not. He included the entire song of Deborah and Barak because he deemed it important for Israel to remember the details and to celebrate the accomplishments of their victory over the Canaanites. As we see repeatedly, the Bible writers never waste words. Recording so many words in this song of victory indicates the importance the author places on it. In that respect, it rivals the song of Moses. In addition, both songs describe the chariots of the opposition being carried away by surging waters. For the ancient reader, the comparison would be clear and therefore likely intended by the author.

If that were not enough to establish Deborah's importance, the final words of Judges 5 give the results of her judgeship and seal her significance—Israel "had peace forty years."

When the monarchy comes to Israel, only a few of the kings will reign as long as Deborah. David and Solomon, who represent the Golden Age of the kingdom of Israel, each reigned for forty years.

So in Deborah we have a judge who led the people to a military victory over their enemies, a deliverance being compared to the deliverance of Israel through the Red Sea, and who then served as judge during forty years of peace. There is nothing negative attributed to her—a record unparalleled by any of the other judges.

Come to think of it, how many of the judges can you name? We have one entire book dedicated to describing the exploits of the judges, not counting the books of Samuel, which describe the deeds of the last of the judges. Some, no doubt, would probably remember Gideon and Samson. Very few would know the others.

Gideon did rule in peace for forty years, but after his great victory over Midian, he made a memorial out of part of the plunder from those battles, and that memorial became an object of worship: "All Israel prostituted themselves by worshiping it there, and it became a snare to Gideon and his family" (Judges 8:27). And Samson's relatively brief misrule was marked with serious problems.

Of the other judges, only Samuel can claim so great a stature as Deborah, but we often forget the consequences caused by the behavior of his sons. Sadly, despite Samuel's personal piety, his sons' corrupt behavior is a black mark on his legacy.

"When Samuel grew old, he appointed his sons as Israel's leaders. . . . But his sons did not follow his ways. They turned aside after dishonest gain and accepted bribes and perverted justice. So all the elders of Israel gathered together and came to Samuel at Ramah. They said to him, 'You are old, and your sons do not follow your ways; now appoint a king to lead us, such as all the other nations have' " (1 Samuel 8:1, 3–5).

Deborah achieved the ultimate goal of any ruler, as far as the Bible is concerned—to give God's people rest. Success in battle, and peace during her tenure, these are God's response to Deborah's leadership. The inspired writers can give no higher accolade than to say that during his or, as in this case, her tenure, God's people experienced rest. Based on this, we would have to rank Deborah among the greatest of the judges.

Of all the judges, Deborah and Samuel stand out above the rest, making them the "strong partners" as judges of Israel.

The next woman we shall consider has probably the most complex story of all the women in Scripture.

SIX

RUTH
AMAZING FAITH

"It was the best of times, it was the worst of times . . ." These famous words begin Charles Dickens's book, *A Tale of Two Cities*, foreshadowing a story of stark contrasts. Dickens might have been describing the story of Ruth. The contrasts in her story are just as striking, for though no actual violence occurs, there is death and bitterness, grief and recrimination, and also new life and rejoicing, celebration and praise. In fact, life and death launch the story. For the observant reader, the Ruth narrative contains layer after layer of irony and reversal, as in Dickens's great story. The drama is subdued yet intense in Ruth's story.

On its surface, the story of Ruth is a charming romance. A famine leaves three women, a mother and two daughters-in-law, widowed. Bereaved and bitter—she even says her new name is "Mara," "bitter"—the older woman determines to return to the land of her birth and die there. She encourages the younger women to remain where they are, where the prospects of finding a husband will be better. One daughter-in-law agrees, reluctantly; but the other one, intensely loyal, vows to stay with the older woman, and die in what is to her a foreign land. After a series of adventures, the plucky young widow finds a husband and provides a legacy for her mother-in-law. That's the romance. But even that just scratches the surface.

As you may remember, in the story of Jochebed and Moses we encountered the Betrothal Narrative story framework. On the surface, the entire book of Ruth is a Betrothal Narrative with many twists and turns. We've also looked at the Barren Woman and the Rejected Cornerstone. They show up in the story of Ruth as well. In fact, the story of Ruth is so intricately crafted that we will encounter all these and two more story frameworks: the Sojourner and the Firstborn Reversal. The author combines all of these and more into an incredibly rich narrative tapestry. They will emerge as we dig under the surface of the story.

"In the days when the judges judged, there was a famine in the land. A certain man of Bethlehem Judah went to live in the country of Moab, he, and his wife, and his two sons. The name of the man was Elimelech, and the name of his wife Naomi. The names of his two sons were Mahlon and Chilion, Ephrathites of Bethlehem Judah. They came into the country of Moab, and lived there" (Ruth 1:1, 2, WEB).

This in itself is a familiar series of events. Famine drove Jacob and his sons to Egypt. They were saved from starvation but ended up enslaved, so their exile was both good and bad. Famine drives Elimelech and his family to Moab. But their exile appears only to have bad results.

Barrenness and Bitterness

"Elimelech, Naomi's husband, died; and she was left with her two sons. They took for themselves wives of the women of Moab. The name of the one was Orpah, and the name of the other was Ruth. They lived there about ten years. Mahlon and Chilion both died, and the woman was bereaved of her two children and of her husband" (verses 3, 4, WEB).

Here we encounter the first hint of the many ironies and twists this story has in store for us. Naomi has become, *late in life*, a Barren Woman. For the ancient reader this is ironic beyond words. Israelites were forbidden to intermarry with foreigners, but especially those from Moab. It was the Moabites who summoned Balaam to curse the Israelites, and when his curses failed, he counseled the Moabites to seduce the Israelites into immorality. The Moabites worshiped a fertility god, Chemosh, which included ritual prostitution and infant sacrifice, both of which were abominations to Israel's God. Further, the Moabites were tainted from the beginning, since Moab, for whom the nation was named, was the fruit of the incestuous union of Lot and his elder daughter after the destruction of Sodom and Gomorrah.

On the surface this teaches a painful lesson. Naomi moves with her husband and sons into a land where fertility is worshiped and licentious behavior is common, and *there* she becomes barren. She has a husband and two sons when she moves to Moab but loses them all there. In case the reader misses the point, the narrator has Naomi explain it when she and her daughters-in-law approach the land of Israel:

"Naomi said, 'Go back, my daughters. Why do you want to go with me? Do I still have sons in my womb, that they may be your husbands? Go back, my daughters, go your way; for I am too old to have a husband. If I should say,

"I have hope," if I should even have a husband tonight, and should also bear sons; would you then wait until they were grown? Would you then refrain from having husbands? No, my daughters, for it grieves me seriously for your sakes, for Yahweh's hand has gone out against me' " (verses 11–13, WEB).

She thus declares herself barren at God's hands. She has no sons to offer, nor is it possible that she will have any at some later date, and even if she did, it would be too long before they could grow to manhood. Her destitution is complete, and anyone depending on her would share her deprivation.

"God is punishing me," Naomi tells them. "No reason for you to suffer too." And she knows, even if she does not say it, that Moabite women may not be properly respected in Israel. Orpah, not unreasonably, follows Naomi's advice and turns her steps back to Moab. But despite Naomi's warning, Ruth remains determined to stay with her mother-in-law. Her promise is quite startling:

"Don't urge me to leave you, and to return from following you, for where you go, I will go; and where you stay, I will stay. Your people will be my people, and your God my God. Where you die, I will die, and there I will be buried" (verses 16, 17, WEB).

Ruth here pledges no less than to share a life of censure, deprivation, poverty, and death far from her homeland, in order to stay with her mother-in-law. This is an especially amazing promise, because Naomi herself is, at that time, deeply unhappy.

"So they both went until they came to Bethlehem. When they had come to Bethlehem, all the city was excited about them, and they asked, 'Is this Naomi?' She said to them, 'Don't call me Naomi. Call me Mara; for the Almighty has dealt very bitterly with me. I went out full, and Yahweh has brought me home again empty' " (verses 19–21, WEB).

Naomi means "pleasant"; Mara means "bitter"; and names throughout the Bible reflect character. Naomi identifies the object of her bitterness, again affirming her barrenness, believing it a judgment from God: *I went out full, and Yahweh has brought me home again empty.*

Betrothal Narrative

"So Naomi returned, and Ruth the Moabitess, her daughter-in-law, with her, who returned out of the country of Moab. They came to Bethlehem in the beginning of barley harvest" (verse 22, WEB).

Note the interesting wording: Ruth *returned* out of the country of Moab. A well-known popular song describes someone "going home, to a place he'd never been before." That's very much what is happening here. Ruth, born in Moab, has never been to Israel before but is said to have *returned*. That will be a continuing theme in the book, as pointed out by Robert Alter: *"Ruth is said to have 'returned' to Bethlehem, an alien place to her, when it is only her mother-in-law who has really returned. But we get a progressive sense that she is actually coming back to the unknown homeland of her new destiny.*"[1]

"Coming back to the unknown homeland of her new destiny." This is a new twist to the "stranger in a strange land" (which will be his home) motif, which is part of the Sojourner story framework. The ultimate Sojourner is Jesus. He comes from another place, heaven, sent by God on a specific mission. In addition to Jesus, Abraham, Joseph, Daniel, and a number of others are examples of Sojourners. So we have here the beginnings of an idea that Ruth might be such a one. Despite being born in Moab, she may have been sent by God—though that is not yet clear—to Israel for some important purpose.

"Ruth the Moabitess said to Naomi, 'Let me now go to the field, and glean among the ears of grain. . . . She went, and came and gleaned in the field after the reapers; and she happened to come to the portion of the field belonging to Boaz, who was of the family of Elimelech' " (Ruth 2:2, 3, WEB).

This was Israel's poverty program, instituted by God. Farmers and orchard and vineyard owners were to leave specific portions of the crop ungathered. This would be available to the truly poor, but it would not be delivered to them. Instead, the poor went to the fields, orchards, and vineyards and gathered what had been left for them. Naomi and Ruth are poor, so Ruth offers to go and gather what she can for their sustenance. She quickly comes to the attention of Boaz.

"Then Boaz said to his servant who was set over the reapers, 'Whose young lady is this?' " (verse 5, WEB).

I mentioned that the Betrothal Narrative serves as the framework for the whole story of Ruth. Remember that the components include the protagonist going to a foreign land, to a well where he meets a girl or girls. Someone offers to draw water, and then the girl or girls rush back home, telling their father about it. The stranger is invited to share a meal, after which a betrothal takes place. Biblical authors vary and alter specific parts of such a framework, and in Ruth we have major alterations already.

First, instead of a prospective groom, we have a widow; instead of a male, she's female; instead of a Hebrew, she's a Moabite; the "far country"—and to her it *is* a far country—is the Land of Promise. Perhaps you're thinking that's just too many variations. Maybe this isn't actually a Betrothal Narrative. After all, the prospective couple—he an older, confirmed bachelor, she a Moabite widow—meet in a field, no well or water in sight.

"Then Boaz said to Ruth, 'Listen, my daughter. Don't go to glean in another field, and don't go from here, but stay here close to my maidens. Let your eyes be on the field that they reap, and go after them. Haven't I commanded the young men not to touch you? When you are thirsty, go to the vessels, and drink from that which the young men have drawn' " (verses 8, 9, WEB).

But then, when we are about to conclude that it is not a Betrothal Narrative, there's the water, just as the framework requires, although in this case it is drawn by young men rather than young women. That's one of the delights of this fascinating tale. The author cleverly weaves this Betrothal Narrative with contrasting strands, both to highlight the importance of Ruth and to delight his readers with the creativity with which the conventional story is reversed. That should not surprise us, because from beginning to end the Bible is a book of reversals. We live in an upside-down world, the Bible tells us. We live in a world where sin abounds, hardship and corruption surround us, and death is the fate of all. The reversal stories demonstrate God's power to continually turn this upside-down world right-side up again. The evil one may have temporary sway, but even as we witness the death and destruction, it begins to fade away.

Boaz's kindness amazes the humble Ruth. "Then she fell on her face, and bowed herself to the ground, and said to him, 'Why have I found favor in your sight, that you should take knowledge of me, since I am a foreigner?' " (verse 10, WEB).

Surprised by Boaz's generosity and his concern for her personally, Ruth inquires as to the cause. Boaz replies with words that at first seem generous and kind but not especially profound:

"Boaz answered her, 'I have been fully told about all that you have done to your mother-in-law since the death of your husband, and how you have left your father and your mother, and the land of your birth, and have come to a people that you didn't know before. May Yahweh repay your work, and a full reward be given to you from Yahweh, the God of Israel, under whose wings you have come to take refuge' " (verses 11, 12, WEB).

Even the casual reader will see the grace and eloquence in this speech. But it's easy to miss the amazing comparison hidden here. Compare these two passages:

Genesis 12:1	Ruth 2:11
Now Yahweh said to Abram, "Leave your country, and your relatives, and your father's house, and go to the land that I will show you."	Boaz answered her, ". . . you have left your father and your mother, and the land of your birth, and have come to a people that you didn't know before."

The wording is remarkably similar. A detailed comparison is even more striking.[2]

God directs Abraham to:	Ruth voluntarily:
Leave your country	left . . . the land of [her] birth

| Leave . . . your relatives, and your father's house | left [her] father and [her] mother |
| go to the land that I will show you | [came] to a people that [she] didn't know before |

No wonder Robert Alter calls this passage "a pointed allusion to Abraham."³

And there is yet more. The Betrothal Narrative includes a meal, and here it comes. "At meal time Boaz said to her, 'Come here, and eat some bread, and dip your morsel in the vinegar' " (verse 14, WEB).

In the context of the Betrothal Narrative, it fits well. But in the context of a poor woman gleaning in the field, it is extraordinary. There might be many gleaners in a field, while the owner might be absent, in some other field altogether. But here the owner, Boaz, having singled out Ruth already, invites her to share his meal. No doubt this started tongues to wagging among the laborers. Clearly Boaz had—as we might say—"taken a shine" to Ruth. And the evidence for that only grows.

"When she had risen up to glean, Boaz commanded his young men, saying, 'Let her glean even among the sheaves, and don't reproach her. Also pull out some for her from the bundles, and leave it. Let her glean, and don't rebuke her' " (verses 15, 16, WEB).

Boaz makes it clear to his workers that he wants Ruth to get all the grain she can carry, by allowing her to glean in the main part of the field, not just the corners or edges. And to make sure, they are to take some grain from that already bundled and leave it on the ground where she will find it. This has striking results:

> So she gleaned in the field until evening; and she beat out that which she had gleaned, and it was about an ephah of barley. She took it up, and went into the city. Then her mother-in-law saw what she had gleaned; and she brought out and gave to her that which she had left after she had enough.
>
> Her mother-in-law said to her, "Where have you gleaned today? Where have you worked? Blessed be he who noticed you" (verses 17–19, WEB).

An *ephah* would be approximately two-thirds of a bushel, or about thirty pounds, enough for Naomi to have all she needed and more besides. Naomi immediately knows something extraordinary has taken place; ordinary gleaning would not yield nearly so much. So she inquires as to where Ruth had spent her time. Upon hearing the name Boaz, Naomi informs her daughter-in-law that he is "a close relative to us, one of our near kinsmen."

"Ruth the Moabitess said, 'Yes, he said to me, "You shall stay close to my young men, until they have finished all my harvest" ' " (verse 21, WEB).

"All my harvest . . ." From Boaz's perspective, this achieves two positive outcomes. First, he faces the pleasant prospect of being able to see the charming young woman on a regular basis, and in a manner that will not stimulate gossip. Second, it will assure that Ruth and Naomi will have a more than adequate supply of grain, which he has made clear he desires to provide.

Whether Ruth recognizes the significance of Boaz's relationship to Elimelech or not, Naomi does. At this point, Naomi has no way of knowing for certain whether Boaz is just being kind or whether he is attracted to the young widow, but clearly she is on the alert. Naomi has explicitly identified Boaz as "a near kinsman," indicating her awareness that a levirate marriage might be a possibility. Boaz has no wife, and has demonstrated more than casual interest in Ruth. Even if his primary interest is simple kindness, she knows that can easily blossom into something more.

Naomi was aware of the possible effects of continued close association between a healthy male and a healthy female who enjoy each other's company. In case neither of them is aware of just how strong the attraction between them has become, she shrewdly counsels Ruth to do just as Boaz suggested, to continue to go only to his fields. And the narrator informs us that "she stayed close to the maidens of Boaz, to glean to the end of barley harvest and of wheat harvest; and she lived with her mother-in-law" (verse 23, WEB).

The barley harvest took place in our month of April, the wheat harvest in May. So the relationship between Boaz and Ruth continued for perhaps as long as two months. If their interest in each other has grown, the narrative gives no indication. Boaz shows no intention of changing the status quo, and in that culture, Ruth is limited in what she may do about it. Besides which, her evident humility probably limits even her aspirations. Ruth sees herself as beneath his consideration, as we know from her first words to Boaz: "Why have I found favor in your sight, that you should take knowledge of me, since I am a foreigner?" (verse 10, WEB).

She recognizes the common disdain of Israelites for Moabites and is surprised that such a wealthy and important Israelite would show her kindness. His reply shows that he knows of her devotion to Naomi, and demonstrates nobility that is rare in any age. He sees her *character*, which matters more to him than her *ethnicity*, and bestows this benediction:

"May Yahweh repay your work, and a full reward be given to you from Yahweh, the God of Israel, under whose wings you have come to take refuge" (verse 12, WEB).

Remember those words about taking refuge *under God's wings*. This imagery will be important later on. And in reply she yet again expresses humility. "Let me find favor in your sight, my lord, because you have comforted me, and because you have spoken kindly to your servant, though I am not as one of your servants" (verse 13, WEB).

The words, "I am not as one of your servants," indicates she does not consider herself worthy even to be one of his servants.

The threshing floor

Whatever the causes, after two months of continual close contact, nothing seems to change between Ruth and Boaz. And the season for harvest—and therefore the occasion for the two to be in close contact—will soon come to an end. Naomi decides that the time for action has arrived. We know what she proposed, but what she had in mind—and what really happened that night on the threshing floor—are matters of considerable debate.

Despite his kindness toward Ruth, Boaz does not seem inclined to move their relationship forward. As an outside observer, Naomi sees that the two would make a good couple, even though neither of them seems inclined to take the first step toward that end. She decides to move things along.

"My daughter, shall I not seek rest for you, that it may be well with you? Now isn't Boaz our kinsman, with whose maidens you were? Behold, he will be winnowing barley tonight on the threshing floor" (Ruth 3:1, 2, WEB).

There are several things to note in this seemingly simple passage. Israel in those days was an agricultural society. The book of Ruth repeats the themes of fruitfulness and harvest throughout. The events in the narrative move with the rhythms of threshing and harvesting, of sowing seed and cultivating crops. And here we see it again. Ruth met Boaz during the barley harvest. We have been told that the wheat harvest has concluded, and now he is ready to thresh and winnow the barley. Threshing time, like shearing time, was a time of celebration, feasting, and drinking. In ancient times, every successful crop was cause for celebration. And in a society where they had few means for preserving food long term, feasting generally accompanied successful harvests.

Threshing floors in particular were known for their celebrations—often rather wild ones. So much so that the term "threshing floor" came to be used as a euphemism for what used to be called a "red light district." So the ancient reader wonders just what Naomi has up her sleeve. "Therefore wash yourself, anoint yourself, get dressed, and go down to the threshing floor, but don't make yourself known to the man until he has finished eating and drinking" (verse 3, WEB).

Having Ruth bathe, apply perfume—that's what "anointing" means in this context—and go down to the threshing floor (there's that term again!) only heightens the tension.

"It shall be, when he lies down, that you shall note the place where he is lying. Then you shall go in, uncover his feet, and [lie] down. Then he will tell you what to do" (verse 4, WEB).

If ever an action was calculated to force the issue, this is it. In "uncovering his feet" and lying down next to Boaz, Ruth is essentially offering herself in marriage. There can be no mistaking the meaning of this bold tactic, as Boaz will quickly make clear. Should Boaz accept her offer, their union might be consummated on the spot. Ruth would have found the rest that Naomi sought for her. That's the unspoken message behind the words "he will tell you what to do." Of course, he might refuse, and, if so, he would tell Ruth to leave. She would be spared embarrassment by having gone to him secretly. There remains some risk for Ruth if she follows Naomi's instructions and decides to go to the threshing floor. But Ruth trusts Naomi, and Naomi trusts Boaz—and events will show each woman's trust to be well justified.

"When Boaz had eaten and drunk, and his heart was merry, he went to lie down at the end of the heap of grain" (verse 7, WEB).

The most vulnerable time for the harvest, when thieves and outlaws loved to strike, was the short time after the grain had been threshed and winnowed but before it had been stored away. To safeguard his grain, Boaz places himself right next to it, so that any attempt at theft will waken him. So Ruth runs some risk in that, should he waken suddenly at her approach, he might mistake her for a thief.

The symbolism of Boaz sleeping on the fruits of an abundant harvest cannot be lost on the reader. Clearly, Boaz's fields have been fruitful, which bodes well for his own fertility, and for that of the prospective couple—should they marry. It is in this highly suggestive context that Ruth follows Naomi's instructions to the letter.

"At midnight, the man was startled and turned himself; and behold, a woman lay at his feet. He said, 'Who are you?' She answered, 'I am Ruth your servant. Therefore spread the corner of your garment over your servant; for you are a near kinsman' " (verses 8, 9, WEB).

The word here translated "corner" can also be translated "hem" but in chapter 2 was rendered "wing." Remember when Boaz said, "May Yahweh repay your work, and a full reward be given to you from Yahweh, the God of Israel, under whose wings you have come to take refuge"? The word *wings* comes from the same Hebrew word. Boaz invoked this blessing on Ruth. She now asks that he take her under his "wing," or his protection, as "near kinsman." Near kinsman also has the connotation of "redeemer," since the near kinsman had the right and responsibility to buy back or redeem the land owned by the deceased and to care for his widow. Asking him to "spread the corner of [his] garment over [her]" amounts to a request to become his wife. And identifying him as near kinsman makes it explicit.

So we have a woman—a foreigner from Moab, no less—proposing marriage to a wealthy Israelite. This was a bold move on her part, certainly, and almost shocking in the context of the times. The stunned but gratified Boaz replies in admiration:

"You have shown more kindness in the latter end than at the beginning, because you didn't follow young men, whether poor or rich" (verse 10, WEB).

He considers her young and beautiful and himself to be old and not desirable, and he wonders aloud that she should offer herself to him. He deeply admires the way she has devoted herself to Naomi, her mother-in-law—the "former kindness"—but finds this offer even more astounding.

But there is a problem. "Now it is true that I am a near kinsman," Boaz says. "However, there is a kinsman nearer than I. Stay this night, and in the morning, if he will perform for you the part of a kinsman, good. Let him do the kinsman's duty. But if he will not do the duty of a kinsman for you, then I will do the duty of a kinsman for you, as Yahweh lives" (verses 12, 13, WEB).

Ever meticulous and honorable, Boaz acts to protect Ruth in three separate ways. First, he informs her that another, more closely related kinsman exists, and that he has first right of refusal. Second, he bids her stay the night with him rather than risk returning home alone in the dark. Finally, he tells her to leave before the other workers awake, so no scandal will arise. Anyone seeing her lying with him on the threshing floor would assume the worst. A Moabite—and we know how promiscuous they are—found sleeping with Boaz—*on the threshing floor!* No doubt the gossip would arrive in Bethlehem before they did. Even should they later marry, people would say she had "flung herself at him," a charge that would have more than a little validity, so bold was the move Naomi had instigated Ruth into committing.

"She lay at his feet until the morning, then she rose up before one could discern another. For he said, 'Let it not be known that the woman came to the threshing floor.' He said, 'Bring the mantle that is on you, and hold it.' She held it; and he measured six measures of barley, and laid it on her; then he went into the city" (verses 14, 15, WEB).

Exactly how much six measures of barley amounted to cannot be clearly determined from the text. Six *ephahs* would be about four bushels, nearly two hundred pounds of barley, clearly too much for Ruth to have lifted, much less carried any distance. And the word used here is a verb, as in "*to* measure," rather than a noun "*a* measure." Whatever the actual weight, it represents a significant amount of grain. Boaz wants Ruth, and by extension Naomi, to understand that he recognizes and values the offer made to him. That's why Naomi, after hearing Ruth's comprehensive account of what had taken place at the threshing floor, including the detail that Boaz had gone "into the city," could say with such assurance, "*The man will not rest until he has settled this today.*"

Justice done and seen to be done

Naomi knew what she was talking about. Boaz went to the city with a clear purpose in mind: secure for himself the land of Naomi and the hand of Ruth.

"Now Boaz went up to the gate, and sat down there. Behold, the near kinsman of whom Boaz spoke came by. He said to him, 'Come over here, friend, and sit down!' He turned aside, and sat down. He took ten men of the elders of the city, and said, 'Sit down here,' and they sat down" (Ruth 4:1, 2, WEB).

The ancient reader recognizes this scene immediately. It's like the opening of *Perry Mason* or *Matlock*, or a scene from *Law & Order*—a courtroom, a judge upon the bench, and a waiting jury. A legal proceeding is about to begin; justice will be dispensed. In the ancient world, wise men gathered at the city gate, and individuals brought their petitions to be decided, their disputes settled. Boaz recognizes a timeless truth that sometimes we forget: justice must *be* accomplished and must *be seen* to have been accomplished. This is essential for any society in order to maintain internal order and peace.

The ancient law requires that a young widow receive the care and support of a husband; *justice must be done*. But a procedure exists on how this relief is to be provided and who should provide it, and that procedure must be recognized as fairly administered. *Justice must be seen to have been done*. Boaz has determined to satisfy both requirements. He brings the case before his impromptu jury—the ten elders.

"He said to the near kinsman, 'Naomi, who has come back out of the country of Moab, is selling the parcel of land, which was our brother Elimelech's. I thought I should tell you, saying, "Buy it before those who sit here, and before the elders of my people." If you will redeem it, redeem it; but if you will not redeem it, then tell me, that I may know. For there is no one to redeem it besides you; and I am after you' " (verses 3, 4, WEB).

The author of this story does not name the other near kinsman, thus making clear that he is not a significant player in this narrative. Yes, the man has a choice to make—he *could* be a major character—but his not being named forewarns us that he will not be. Note that in this narrative, the near kinsman appears in the role of the firstborn—that is, according to birth, he is more closely related to Naomi than Boaz, and thus he receives preference. But as mentioned earlier, in Scripture the firstborn almost never actually benefits from that accident of birth. At first, this situation looks as though it will follow the firstborn rule (but don't forget we don't know his name!). Apparently eager to acquire the land for himself, the other near kinsman says, "I will redeem it."

It appears that Naomi's stratagem and Ruth's desire to marry Boaz have failed. But, just as Naomi knows Boaz, Boaz knows his unnamed rival, and at this point he mentions *the rest* of the purchase price:

"Then Boaz said, 'On the day you buy the field from the hand of Naomi, you must buy it also from Ruth the Moabitess, the wife of the dead, to raise up the name of the dead on his inheritance' " (verse 5, WEB).

Here we have a fascinating insight into the whole issue of what we call levirate marriage: "You must buy it *also*," Boaz says, "*from Ruth* the Moabitess." The price of the land, whether in coin, livestock, or other items of value, would go to Elimelech's widow, Naomi, to support her in her old age. But the existence of a marriageable widow, namely Ruth, meant she also must be compensated. And that price consisted of the requirement to give her a son, "to raise up the name of the dead on his inheritance."

The near kinsman had already agreed to pay the first price; the second one, however, posed an insurmountable obstacle in his mind. "The near kinsman said, 'I can't redeem it for myself, lest I endanger my own inheritance' " (verse 6, WEB).

What does he find so daunting about marrying Ruth that it would "endanger" his inheritance? We encountered this before with Onan. It comes down to this: when a man died, his possessions would be divided by the number of living sons, plus one. The firstborn would then receive two of those portions, "the double portion" mentioned several times in Scripture. We don't know how many sons the near kinsman had, or if he had any. If he had sons, and he married Ruth and she bore him a son, two portions of his legacy would go to that child, because he would be considered Elimelech's son. Elimelech had been born before the near kinsman himself, and so his son would receive preference over the near kinsman's first son. If the first kinsman never had other sons, *all* of his possessions would go to Ruth's child. In any case, a significant part of his belongings would go to someone legally recognized as another man's son. He decided not to take that chance.

We do not know whether the near kinsman had other sons or not, but Boaz *did* know. And the way Boaz handled the case, first simply mentioning the land and *then* revealing the required marriage, with its implications for the man's legacy, tells us he had a good idea of how the other man's mind would work. The near kinsman jumped at the chance to buy the land but declined the marriage.

And in so doing, he completes the Firstborn Reversal story framework. Like virtually all of the type-scenes or story frameworks in the book of Ruth, the author has completed the scene, but with a clever twist. Boaz and the near kinsman are not brothers, but as we noted earlier, the near kinsman appears in the role of the firstborn—according to birth, he is more closely related to Naomi than Boaz is, and thus he receives preference. In previous instances in Scripture, the reversal happened in spite of and contrary to the firstborn's wishes: Isaac is preferred over his older brother, Ishmael; Jacob steals his brother's blessing; Reuben loses his blessing by asserting it too soon; and Jacob intentionally confers it on the younger of Joseph's two sons. Here, with appropriate irony, the near kinsman *declines* his firstborn privilege.

At this point, the fascinating tale approaches its conclusion. Indeed, the way we usually tell the tale, once Boaz secures the right to marry Ruth, we focus on the fact that she was the mother of Obed, the grandfather of King David. But we skip over some of the delicious details the author has worked so hard for us to appreciate. We have essentially concluded the Betrothal Narrative and the Firstborn Reversal, but several other loose ends remain.

We said that justice must be done, and justice must be seen to have been done. By bringing the case to the elders at the city gate, Boaz satisfies both those requirements. And the near kinsman will finalize it formally. Today, though, when we sign a contract, we typically have the idea of shaking hands to formally close a deal. Ancient Israel had a similar but slightly different custom.

"Now this was the custom in former time in Israel concerning redeeming and concerning exchanging, to confirm all things: a man took off his shoe, and gave it to his neighbor; and this was the way of legalizing transactions in Israel. So the near kinsman said to Boaz, 'Buy it for yourself,' then he took off his shoe" (verses 7, 8, WEB).

Many times, we have little or no direct evidence of when a biblical book was written, relative to the events in the book, but Ruth is an exception. We know it was written well after the events related, long enough that at least one custom had changed and perhaps been largely forgotten. We know that because the author feels it necessary to intrude into the sequence of events and explain the custom of passing the shoe: *"Now this was the custom in former time in Israel . . ."*

In our own day, documents often need to be witnessed or notarized; the claims of one individual are not enough. And so it was in Ruth's day. Boaz, meticulous in detail, makes certain to meet that requirement as well.

"Boaz said to the elders, and to all the people, 'You are witnesses today, that I have bought all that was Elimelech's, and all that was Chilion's and Mahlon's, from the hand of Naomi. Moreover Ruth the Moabitess, the wife of Mahlon, I have purchased to be my wife, to raise up the name of the dead on his inheritance, that the name of the dead may not be cut off from among his brothers, and from the gate of his place. You are witnesses today' " (verses 9, 10, WEB).

The crowd acknowledges the closing of the deal, and then adds several interesting things: "All the people who were in the gate, and the elders, said, 'We are witnesses. May Yahweh make the woman who has come into your house like Rachel and like Leah, which both built the house of Israel; and treat you worthily in Ephrathah, and be famous in Bethlehem. Let your house be like the house of Perez, whom Tamar bore to Judah, of the offspring which Yahweh will give you by this young woman' " (verses 11, 12).

Because the crowd here compares Ruth to Rachel and Leah who "built the house of Israel," and Tamar who was in the royal line, many assume that this speech did not in fact happen, that it was inserted at a later date to make the whole episode look prophetic. And we cannot deny that possibility. After all, the book of Ruth does begin with the words, "In the days when the judges judged," and we noted that the custom of "passing the shoe" had ceased to be practiced. So we know that this account was written later. But that does not mean these words were not originally spoken. It is an unfortunate habit of mind to assume that because a story was not written until some years after it occurred, that the details *must* have been manufactured.

It is quite possible that many of these words were spoken at virtually every wedding in those days. I do not need a written record of every wedding anniversary or birthday celebration to report with confidence that each year people wished me "many more," but neither would it be inaccurate to include such well wishes in relating any of those events. So it is quite possible that people said the words reported in this account along with many others, and the author selected these to emphasize his point. The fact that these were not the *only* words spoken at the time—and surely they were not—does not make it any less true that these words were spoken. And it is often true in our own lives that when we look back at significant events in our past, we realize that some words spoken at the time were truer than we could have imagined.

Mother of the Faithful

Wasting no time, the narrator declares: "So Boaz took Ruth, and she became his wife; and he went in to her, and Yahweh enabled her to conceive, and she bore a son" (verse 13, WEB).

We noted before, in the story of Tamar, that the Old Testament writers always recognize that when conception occurs, it occurs because God makes it possible. Here the author makes it explicit: "Yahweh enabled her to conceive." So Ruth becomes pregnant and gives birth to a son. And here we encounter a delightful twist on one of our story frameworks.

Early on, we mentioned that Naomi appears in this narrative as the Barren Woman. Although she had borne two sons, when this story begins, she has become, by her own declaration, a barren woman. She has no sons to offer her widowed daughters-in-law, nor will she have any more in the future. Ruth has made her a grandmother, but does that change her status as a mother? She still has no sons. Or does she?

"The women said to Naomi, 'Blessed be Yahweh, who has not left you today without a near kinsman. Let his name be famous in Israel. He shall be to you a restorer of life, and sustain you in your old age, for your daughter-in-law, who loves you, who is better to you than seven sons, has given birth to him' " (verses 14, 15, WEB).

"Your daughter-in-law . . . is better to you than seven sons." Seven being the number of maturity, completion, and, yes, perfection, the women declare Ruth to be better than the perfect son. Does this make Naomi no longer barren? Sort of. But there's more.

"Naomi took the child, and laid him in her bosom, and became nurse to it. The women, her neighbors, gave him a name, saying, 'A son is born to Naomi' " (verses 16, 17).

There it is. The narrator simply refuses to let us miss the point. "A son is born to Naomi!" And by "becom[ing] nurse" to the child, she is "mothering" him. This completes the Barren Woman framework, as God gives Naomi a daughter-in-law who refuses to abandon her, and who ultimately makes her a mother again.

As we have seen, Bible writers love to repeat, mirror, or echo earlier themes, scenarios, and phrases. They do this to remind us of God's saving actions in the past and show us that He continues to work in the same ways throughout history and in the present. No, God does not woodenly repeat Himself, but as a great composer writes a symphony, He repeats variations on melodies and phrases—higher, lower, inverted, sideways, or in a new key. We recognize the familiar tune, but we also appreciate the creativity of the new variations. Joseph and Daniel, both captives, were given the power to interpret dreams, and both rose to prominence in their exile. Both will give hope to God's people, and both will help preserve them. It is the same basic storyline but with variations. Think of Joseph in Egypt, sold by his brothers; Daniel in Babylon, conquered by Nebuchadnezzar.

And in the story of Ruth, we have seen several story frameworks repeat themselves with charming variations: the Barren Woman, the Firstborn Reversal, the Betrothal Narrative. One has already been hinted at: the Sojourner.

Boaz explicitly compared Ruth to the first Sojourner mentioned in Scripture, Abraham. In the Sojourner story, God sends or summons someone to a foreign land, not for a time but for a lifetime. Abraham left the land of his birth and went to a land God promised to show him. Even at the end of his life, though, Abraham has not yet come into possession of the land of promise. When beloved Sarah dies, Abraham has to haggle, and ultimately pay a high price, to purchase a tiny fragment of that promised inheritance—a cave in which to bury his wife.

Joseph and Daniel are Sojourners, taken to foreign lands to fulfill God's design. And though they help provide deliverance and eventual return for God's people, they die far from their homelands. Jesus is the ultimate Sojourner, by leaving heaven to dwell as a human with humans, dying at our hands, and being buried in a borrowed grave.

Ruth, born in Moab, sojourns in Israel, where, as she tells Naomi, she will die and be buried. And so she does.

The remaining story framework, the Rejected Cornerstone, we see in both Ruth and Boaz. The near kinsman explicitly rejects Ruth to preserve his inheritance—ironically, because his inheritance disappears anyway. We know neither his name nor the names of any children he might have had. Ruth's son, however, takes his place in the lineage of David and ultimately of Christ Himself.

Why does the biblical author employ so many of these story frameworks in the narrative of Ruth? He does so to ensure we don't miss the point that in this widow from Moab, God is working in many of the ways He employed with various important figures in the Bible before her. This cumulative use of all these techniques tells us the author wants the reader to realize how mightily God is at work in the life of this one woman.

Boaz, the text implies, is older than Ruth, and we know of no other wife. Despite the fact that he possessed a kind, loving nature, and considerable wealth, he had remained single. We do not know why, but it may be that, just as Ruth's Moabite ethnicity made her suspect, perhaps his own ancestry was considered questionable. He was, after all, the son of a well-known prostitute—Rahab of Jericho. Whatever the cause, he appears to be rejected also. Great literature, we are told, is usually rich in irony. By that standard, or any other, the book of Ruth ranks as a masterpiece.

On the one hand, as Boaz tacitly declares, Ruth's match is Abraham. If he is the "Father of the Faithful," then Ruth, whose faith mirrors that of Abraham, must be the "Mother of the Faithful."

Ruth demonstrates a faith not only as great as Abraham's, but her challenge—and therefore the faith required to meet it—is far greater than the patriarch's. Abraham had a large family, many servants, and the wealth of flocks and herds. Sarah had Abraham, with all his resources, to provide for her.

Ruth had nothing—in some ways, less than nothing. She was a widow supporting an older widow, with no flocks, herds, or crops. And when Boaz makes this comparison to Abraham, she is in the midst of the most menial of tasks: gleaning the leavings of a harvest, so that she and Naomi can subsist. Ruth's faith, her self-sacrifice, and her sweet demeanor in the face of all these hardships surely qualify her as "Mother of the Faithful."

Yet in another way, Ruth's true match must be Boaz himself. In Ruth and Boaz we have an odd couple indeed. An older man, the son of a prostitute, who marries a woman from the licentious country of Moab; yet God blesses their union with a son whose name will live forever! Clearly these two are "strong partners" for each other. Even so, why rank Boaz so highly? Several of the other women have married great men, or had sons whose names live on, yet we have not ranked their consorts to be nearly as great as the women themselves. Here's why.

The greatness of most of the women in this book—women of faith and initiative—comes to be recognized only much later. The biblical authors take pains to demonstrate the greatness of these women precisely because it often went unrecognized, even unnoticed, in their lifetimes. However, Boaz recognizes the stunning beauty of character possessed by this unassuming young woman whom he found gleaning in his field. He says, "I have been fully told about all that you have done to your mother-in-law since the death of your husband, and how you have left your father and your mother, and the land of your birth, and have come to a people that you didn't know before. May Yahweh repay your work, and a full reward be given to you from Yahweh, the God of Israel, under whose wings you have come to take refuge" (Ruth 2:11, 12, WEB).

This beautiful benediction not only blesses her but overflows to his own benefit as well, when she seeks refuge under his "wing." This, too, he recognizes.

"He said, 'You are blessed by Yahweh, my daughter. You have shown more kindness in the latter end than at the beginning, because you didn't follow young men, whether poor or rich' " (Ruth 3:10, WEB).

Elsewhere, I have written that "marriage is all we know of heaven." Contemplating the spiritual beauty of both Ruth and Boaz, it appears that this truly was "a match made in heaven." Yet how strange it is to call it such: a bachelor, son of a prostitute, and a widow from a licentious culture, both rejected by others—a match made in heaven? How ironic! And how like God, who exalts every valley, makes low every mountain, who declares good news to the poor, sight to the blind, cleansing to sinners, and healing to the brokenhearted! Yes, these two are just exactly the sort of match heaven makes.

---

1. Alter, *The Art of Biblical Narrative*, 70; emphasis added.
2. Actually, Ruth resists Naomi's efforts to prevent her from these actions.
3. Alter, *The Art of Biblical Narrative*, 71.

SEVEN

HANNAH
Nobody From Nowhere

Times were desperate in Israel—endless border skirmishes with the Philistines; corrupt priests extorting from worshipers and taking sexual favors from women (see 1 Samuel 2:22). Everyone knows that the high priest, Eli, is unable to control his sons.

The rot in Israel runs deep, but in some places the conflict is personal rather than national. Our story transpires in one of these places. It begins with one woman's anguish.

"Now there was a certain man ... and his name was Elkanah, ... an Ephraimite. He had two wives. The name of one was Hannah, and the name of other Peninnah. Peninnah had children, but Hannah had no children" (1 Samuel 1:1, 2, WEB).

"Hannah had no children." We have seen this situation before in Scripture. Two wives, and one has children, the other does not. In a culture where fertility is the basis of wealth, the childless woman feels worthless.

"This man went up out of his city from year to year to worship and to sacrifice to Yahweh of Armies in Shiloh. The two sons of Eli, Hophni and Phinehas, priests to Yahweh, were there. When the day came that Elkanah sacrificed, he gave to Peninnah his wife, and to all her sons and her daughters, portions; but to Hannah he gave a double portion, for he loved Hannah, but Yahweh had shut up her womb" (verses 3–5, WEB).

Another complicating factor: as so often happens in these stories, the wife without children is the one the husband loves. "To Hannah he gave a double portion." By now, you recognize that this double portion is the one belonging to the firstborn. Elkanah tries to make up to Hannah for her barrenness, but it has the opposite effect. For Hannah, it emphasizes what she sees as her failure, and it infuriates Penninah, who reckons herself as undervalued—because of Hannah.

"Her rival provoked her severely, to irritate her, because Yahweh had shut up her womb. As he did so year by year, when she went up to Yahweh's house. Her rival provoked her; therefore she wept, and didn't eat" (verses 6, 7, WEB,).

This, too, we have seen before. The fertile wife seeing the affection her husband displays for "that other woman," experiences jealousy and pain, which she tries to mitigate by taking it out on her sister-wife. We see that with Hagar and Sarah, with Leah and Rachel, and now we see it with Penninah and Hannah. Of course Penninah does not do this openly, where Elkanah would be angered. And Elkanah does not realize that his demonstration of preference only makes matters worse. An outside observer immediately understands Hannah's dread of the annual pilgrimage to make sacrifice. But Elkanah, oblivious to all this, and specifically as to how his actions exacerbate the situation, cannot understand. He must be thinking, "What is *wrong* with this woman?"

"Elkanah her husband said to her, 'Hannah, why do you weep? Why don't you eat? Why is your heart grieved? Am I not better to you than ten sons?' " (verse 8, WEB).

Why does he say *ten* sons? One would expect seven, the number of perfection and completion. Remember that the women of Bethlehem declared to Naomi that Ruth, "your daughter-in-law, who loves you . . . is better to you than seven sons." Ruth, they said, was better than the perfect son. It seems natural that Elkanah would say the same—"Am I not better to you than 'the perfect son'?" But the author pointedly records that he says *ten*. Why?

We have already identified Elkanah as "an Ephraimite." In Israel, tribal identity matters. There were twelve tribes, however, not ten. So once again, why does Elkanah say ten instead of twelve? Elkanah is likely reminding Hannah about the story of Leah and Rachel. Remember, Jacob had two wives. By Leah he had six sons; by the handmaids, Bilhah and Zilpah, he had two sons each. At that point, Jacob had *ten* sons. Only after this did Rachel conceive and eventually bear two sons. Ten sons and two sons. "Am I not better to you than ten sons?" Even though all the other women bore Jacob ten sons, he loved Rachel more. Elkanah appears to be saying, "I love you as Jacob loved Rachel."

This is cold comfort to a woman who wants to be a mother. Hannah is the Barren Woman. Because we recognize this story framework, we anticipate the likely positive outcome. The delight in these narratives is in the details, in how the expected outcome takes place—or is frustrated. And Hannah would not be in this book if she did not take the initiative, if she did not seize or create opportunity.

"So Hannah rose up after they had finished eating and drinking in Shiloh. Now Eli the priest was sitting on his seat by the doorpost of Yahweh's temple.

Out of the deep distress of her soul, Hannah prayed to Yahweh, weeping bitterly. She vowed a vow, and said, 'Yahweh of Armies, if you will indeed look at the affliction of your servant, and remember me, and not forget your servant, but will give to your servant a boy, then I will give him to Yahweh all the days of his life, and no razor shall come on his head' " (verses 9–12, WEB).

If you thought that saying this story "begins with one woman's anguish," was an overstatement, look at this prayer. Describing "the affliction of your servant," she asks explicitly for a son, which she will then *give up!* Further, she has pledged that the son will be a Nazarite, a special calling described to Moses in Numbers 6 (for purposes of space I abbreviate):

> "When either man or woman shall make a special vow, the vow of a Nazirite, to separate himself to Yahweh, he shall separate himself from wine and strong drink . . . vinegar of wine, or vinegar of fermented drink, . . . any juice of grapes, nor [shall he] eat fresh grapes or dried. . . . He shall eat nothing that is made of the grapevine, from the seeds even to the skins. . . . No razor shall come on his head, until the days are fulfilled. . . . He shall let the locks of the hair of his head grow long. . . . He shall not go near a dead body. . . . All the days of his separation he is holy to Yahweh" (Numbers 6:1–8, WEB).

The vow of the Nazirite could be for a set time, usually several months. But Hannah has set the time at "all the days of his life"! She asks a lot of God; she also offers to give up a great deal.

We know the burden of Hannah's heart because the inspired author tells us, but she does not parade her affliction, nor does she seek sympathy from one and all. Suffering has not made her a bitter complainer. Even in prayer she remains silent.

"As she continued praying before Yahweh, Eli saw her mouth. Now Hannah spoke in her heart. Only her lips moved, but her voice was not heard. Therefore Eli thought she was drunk. Eli said to her, 'How long will you be drunk? Get rid of your wine!' " (1 Samuel 1:12–14, WEB).

What an unexpected turn in the story framework of the Barren Woman! Usually when a barren woman encounters a priest, a prophet, or angel—any messenger of God—the messenger assures her that God has heard her petition; that she will conceive and have a son. But here, with Hannah in fervent prayer, she encounters Eli, high priest and judge of Israel, who immediately concludes that she must be inebriated. As often happens, this tells us more about Eli's expectations than it does about Hannah.

Once again, we see rich irony. Hannah has pledged that her son will never touch strong drink; and as she makes that vow, Eli suspects her of being drunk.

That's because drunkenness and debauchery had become so commonplace, even near the tabernacle, that Eli *expected* to see it. If we did not realize it before, this exchange alone warns us of the desperate situation Israel finds itself in.

"Hannah answered, 'No, my lord, I am a woman of a sorrowful spirit. I have not been drinking wine or strong drink, but I poured out my soul before Yahweh. Don't consider your servant a wicked woman; for I have been speaking out of the abundance of my complaint and my provocation' " (verses 15, 16, WEB).

What a lovely expression: "I have not been drinking wine . . . but I poured out my soul." Remembering that Hebrew poetry features mirrored ideas rather than mirrored sounds, we recognize this as poetic. It even touches cynical old Eli, who now—*after* being rebuked by this woman's quiet piety, and not knowing how prophetically he speaks—performs his role, haltingly, as the messenger who announces the end of barrenness.

"Then Eli answered, 'Go in peace; and may the God of Israel grant your petition that you have asked of him' " (verse 17, WEB).

As John would say of Caiphas many years hence, we say of Eli: "He, being the High Priest . . . prophesied." God did indeed grant her petition.

"When the time had come, Hannah conceived, and bore a son; and she named him Samuel, saying, 'Because I have asked him of Yahweh' " (verse 20, WEB).

The name Samuel means "God has heard."

"The man Elkanah, and all his house, went up to offer to Yahweh the yearly sacrifice, and his vow. But Hannah didn't go up; for she said to her husband, 'Not until the child is weaned; then I will bring him, that he may appear before Yahweh, and stay there forever' " (verses 21, 22).

Quiet in suffering, Hannah remains gracious in success. Some might be tempted to go up to the tabernacle and flaunt her child. But Hannah does not. The scene of her bitter suffering will be one of joy mixed too soon with sorrow. She will bring her treasured child to the tabernacle—and leave him there. She both rejoices that the Lord has granted her a child and grieves because they must part. As it would be for any parent, some of her heart remains there with him, and he never leaves her thoughts.

"Samuel ministered before Yahweh, being a child, clothed with a linen ephod. Moreover, his mother made him a little robe, and brought it to him from year to year, when she came up with her husband to offer the yearly sacrifice" (1 Samuel 2:18, WEB). Every year she makes a robe for Samuel, each year a little larger. Stitch by stitch, week by week she sews the robe for her son who is no longer in her home but is always in her heart.

Belatedly, Eli recognizes the hand of God upon Hannah and consciously performs his prophetic function: "Eli blessed Elkanah and his wife, and said, 'May Yahweh give you offspring from this woman for the petition which was asked of Yahweh.' Then they went to their own home. Yahweh visited Hannah, and she conceived, and bore three sons and two daughters" (verses 20, 21, WEB).

In some ways, this seems a simple story. After all, there are many barren women, both in Scripture and in real life. However, in most of these stories that end positively, God retains the initiative. Already we have encountered three barren women who took the initiative: Tamar, Naomi, and now Hannah. In each case, God expressed His approval by granting their desires—and more. More, because Tamar does not just have a child, but she becomes progenitor of Christ, as does Naomi. Though Hannah does not join them in Christ's lineage, there is a different reward for her. Elkanah is from the tribe of Ephraim, not Judah. Hannah's child becomes a priest—even though not a Levite—and one of the greatest judges.

And though Samuel is not in the kingly line, he becomes the anointer of kings. Ordinarily, royalty is conferred at birth, by virtue of being born the son of a king. Neither Saul nor David were born the son of a king. Samuel becomes father by proxy to both Saul and David, for it is he, through anointing, who confers royalty upon them. And Hannah's petition makes all this possible.

Samuel is not only one of the greatest—and the last—of the judges, but he also begins his duties as judge at an early age. This is Hannah's story, not Samuel's, so we will omit some of the details. But we all remember how God called Samuel's name as the boy slept. When eventually Eli realized it was God speaking to Samuel and instructed him how to respond, God gave the young boy this message to deliver to the high priest:

> Yahweh said to Samuel, "Behold, I will do a thing in Israel, at which both the ears of everyone who hears it will tingle. In that day I will perform against Eli all that I have spoken concerning his house, from the beginning even to the end. For I have told him that I will judge his house forever, for the iniquity which he knew, because his sons brought a curse on themselves, and he didn't restrain them. Therefore I have sworn to the house of Eli, that the iniquity of Eli's house shall not be removed with sacrifice or offering forever" (1 Samuel 3:11–14, WEB).

These are fearful tidings for anyone to deliver; all the more so for a child. And he must tell these terrible judgments of the high priest to his face! God had communicated these things directly to Eli previously. Why does He now repeat them through Samuel? Because, young as he is, Samuel has become the judge of Israel. Sending this message through Samuel ratifies the boy's calling and status, and it signals the passing of authority from the old priest to the young boy.

"Samuel grew, and Yahweh was with him, and let none of his words fall to the ground. All Israel from Dan even to Beersheba knew that Samuel was established to be a prophet of Yahweh. Yahweh appeared again in Shiloh; for Yahweh revealed himself to Samuel in Shiloh by Yahweh's word" (verses 19–21, WEB).

Eli still lives, but he no longer serves as judge. The young Samuel has taken his place, and in the next chapter of 1 Samuel, Eli and his sons die. Samuel will stand out as judge, even among such worthies as Gideon and Samson. Indeed, "Yahweh . . . let none of his [Samuel's] words fall to the ground." An amazing testimony.

We do not know the names of any of Elkanah's other children, only Samuel. Samuel was indeed "better than ten sons," and all because of Hannah's prayers.

It is these prayers that determine Hannah's "strong partner," the match for her role as a woman who took the initiative. Later, a figure will arise at a time when corruption has infected Israel's leadership, and this man, a nobody from nowhere, will initiate, through his prayers, an amazing reformation in Israel. Oddly enough, it is the apostle James who tells us how this great movement began: "Elijah was a man with a nature like ours, and he prayed earnestly that it might not rain, and it didn't rain on the earth for three years and six months. He prayed again, and the sky gave rain, and the earth produced its fruit" (James 5:17, 18, WEB).

Elijah, a "nobody from nowhere"? Actually, yes. We have no information about Elijah, his parents, or what tribe he is from. Although he is called Elijah the Tishbite, we do not know if that tells us his hometown or a nickname, like Honest Abe. He appears suddenly at the court of Ahab and disappears almost as suddenly. After a time of less than five years, he departs the earth on a chariot of fire. So far as we know, he has neither famous ancestors or children, nor does he come from a famous city. In human terms, he's a nobody from nowhere.

Elijah, regarded as the greatest of the prophets, whose prayers brought about reformation in Israel, provides an apt match for Hannah. Her prayers made her the mother of one of the greatest judges, who reformed Israel and anointed kings.

And that, it seems to me, is the ultimate message of Hannah. When we read that "the fervent prayer of a righteous man availeth much," we might assume that the righteous man or woman in question must be *somebody*. A prophet, a pastor, a teacher, an elder—somebody we consider important. But Hannah's story tells us that the fervent prayers of any faithful person—even a nobody from nowhere—can change history.

EIGHT

ABIGAIL
WORTHY OF A KING

This is *not* the beginning of the story: "One of the young men told Abigail, Nabal's wife, saying, 'Behold, David sent messengers out of the wilderness to greet our master; and he insulted them.... Now therefore know and consider what you will do; for evil is determined against our master, and against all his house; for he is such a worthless fellow that one can't speak to him'" (1 Samuel 25:14, 17, WEB).

It *is* the beginning for Abigail. Perhaps you have had this happen to you: influential people in your life take a number of ill-advised or foolish actions without your knowledge. By the time you find out, the situation has become a crisis. Abigail learns that four hundred armed men are en route to slaughter all the men and plunder the flocks and herds in Nabal's camp.

Joseph Conrad's words come to mind: *Being a woman is a terribly difficult task, since it consists principally in dealing with men.* Or, too often, as in this case, dealing with the mess men have made of things.

This is Abigail's world. A foolish man, fueled by ego and testosterone, has uttered angry words and provoked a deadly aggressive action. A soft answer or a diplomatic word might have defused the tense situation, but Abigail was not informed, much less consulted, and the man involved was not in the mood to be diplomatic. At this point, his compounded stupidity and pride threaten to destroy her world. Faced with this imminent danger, some women would have dissolved in tears or run to their husband. Others would have escaped into denial. Not Abigail. She takes immediate and decisive action to defuse this potentially lethal confrontation. And she understands the necessary steps because of something else the servant had told her.

ABIGAIL

"One of the young men told Abigail, Nabal's wife, saying, 'Behold, David sent messengers out of the wilderness to greet our master; and he insulted them. But the men were very good to us, and we were not harmed, and we didn't miss anything, as long as we went with them, when we were in the fields. They were a wall to us both by night and by day, all the while we were with them keeping the sheep' " (1 Samuel 25:14-16, WEB).

This may seem strange to us, but it made perfect sense to Abigail. In ancient times, national boundaries were largely unmarked and mostly unguarded. Fortified cities controlled major travel routes, but those living in the long distances in between could not depend upon the royal army for protection. Cross-border raids were common, as bands of men without property made their living by stealing livestock, grain, and even women from undefended herdsmen and farmers. The servant girl who helped save Namaan was taken in such a raid.

Abigail lived in just such an area, for we are told of her husband: "There was a man in Maon, whose possessions were in Carmel; and the man was very great. He had three thousand sheep and a thousand goats" (1 Samuel 25:2, WEB).

The Carmel ridge runs from the Mediterranean southeast toward the plain of Jezreel in Galilee. The plain of Jezreel was the breadbasket of Israel. Men and nations covet such land and the wealth it can generate. The land was fertile, but it was largely open land, and the royal army could not patrol so vast a frontier. Nabal, with his three thousand sheep and a thousand goats, represented significant wealth and, being in a remote area, provided a tempting target.

The protection that the king could not provide, entrepreneurs could. Sometimes bands of property-less men camped near the frontiers and acted as private security, discouraging raids across the border and repelling others by force. In return, the protected herdsmen and farmers would gladly supply food and animals as a sort of tribute. It made sense to voluntarily contribute a little to these vigilante security forces to protect them. They would otherwise risk losing all to merciless marauders.

David, after being driven from Saul's court, headed up just such a band of men. The servant's words confirmed to Abigail that David and his men had indeed provided protection. Until now, they had not asked for anything in return. But then something new occurred.

"David heard in the wilderness that Nabal was shearing his sheep" (verse 4, WEB).

As we mentioned in the chapter on Tamar, sheep shearing was the first big event after winter. Nabal would have been with the shearers for some days. Wool merchants would leave Nabal and other herdsmen with cash. Feasting and celebrations occupied owners and servants alike.

David, having been a shepherd in his youth, understood all this, and decided it would be a good time to receive a contribution for the protection he and his men had provided.

"David sent ten young men, and David said to the young men, 'Go up to Carmel, and go to Nabal, and greet him in my name. Tell him, "Long life to you! Peace be to you, and peace be to your house, and peace be to all that you have. Now I have heard that you have shearers. Your shepherds have now been with us, and we didn't harm them, neither was there anything missing from them, all the while they were in Carmel. Ask your young men, and they will tell you. Therefore let the young men find favor in your eyes; for we come on a good day. Please give whatever comes to your hand, to your servants, and to your son David" ' " (verses 5–8, WEB).

This reads very much like a business letter with a formal salutation, a statement of services rendered, and a request for payment—all in very respectful language. Note the shrewd references to shearing and "a good day"—pointing out that Nabal's profit is at least partly due to the protection provided by David and his men. Any reasonable man would gladly and generously respond. But Nabal is not reasonable. The servant said as much to Abigail. The author of this episode in the Bible introduced Nabal this way:

"Now the name of the man was Nabal; and the name of his wife Abigail. This woman was intelligent and had a beautiful face; but the man was surly and evil in his doings."

David's request strikes the right tone: respectful and reasonable. Based on her subsequent actions, we know that if David's delegation had come first to "intelligent and beautiful" Abigail, things would have stayed that way. But they spoke to "surly and evil" Nabal, who lived up to his reputation.

"Nabal answered David's servants, and said, 'Who is David? Who is the son of Jesse? There are many servants who break away from their masters these days. Shall I then take my bread, my water, and my meat that I have killed for my shearers, and give it to men who I don't know where they come from?' " (verses 10, 11, WEB).

A simple refusal would have been grounds for a grievance on David's part, but Nabal doesn't stop there. He expresses his contempt for David. In the words, "Who is David?" you may recognize the echo of Pharaoh's disrespect for God, when he said to Moses, "Who is Yahweh?" The implication in both cases is, "He's nobody compared to me; he is not worth considering."

Even that is not enough. In a direct jab at David's recent escape from Saul's court, Nabal speaks of "many servants who break away from their masters these days." So Nabal belittles David as a renegade runaway servant pretending to be somebody of significance. It's enough to make David's blood boil—and it does. It was surely this final insult that led to David's declaration of war against Nabal.

David's messengers "went back, and came and told him [David] all these words [Nabal's reply]. David said to his men, 'Every man put on his sword!' Every man put on his sword. David also put on his sword. About four hundred men followed David" (verses 12, 13, WEB).

Only at this point does Abigail find out what's going on. Now she has to do something to avert the disaster her husband set in motion.

"Then Abigail hurried and took two hundred loaves of bread, two bottles of wine, five sheep ready dressed, five seahs of parched grain, one hundred clusters of raisins, and two hundred cakes of figs, and laid them on donkeys. She said to her young men, 'Go on before me. Behold, I am coming after you.' But she didn't tell her husband, Nabal" (verses 18, 19, WEB).

The sheer size of the peace offering—for that is exactly what it is—tells us several things. First of all, it gives a further glimpse into Nabal's wealth. As we shall see, Abigail can assemble this massive amount of provender without Nabal noticing it, or reducing his own celebratory feast. Second, baking two hundred loaves of bread by hand would take quite a while, no matter how many servants were employed in the task.

Either David's approach took enough time that she could prepare all this food before she went out to meet him, or it was on hand in preparation for the shearing feast. Given the urgency with which she moved, the latter seems more likely. So David and his men are about to enjoy at least some of Nabal's shearing feast, and the reader gets a hearty serving of irony. Whether it was already prepared or not, even gathering all this food and packing it for travel poses a logistical challenge. Abigail not only manages it, but she accomplishes it quickly enough to intercept David and his raiding party.

This procedure of sending servants ahead with gifts is structured to echo the way Jacob approached Esau, who was also leading four hundred armed men. The gifts, it was hoped, would soften the heart of the wronged one, so that he would be inclined to let the petitioner live—and not exact too strong a punishment.

"Now David had said, 'Surely in vain have I kept all that this fellow has in the wilderness, so that nothing was missed of all that pertained to him. He has returned me evil for good. God do so to the enemies of David, and more also, if I leave of all that belongs to him by the morning light so much as one who urinates on a wall' " (verses 21, 22, WEB).

Again, for added emphasis, we hear the echo of David's original words, this time from his own mouth, and accompanied by the verdict: "He has returned me evil for good."

As punishment, David intends to kill every male—he uses the graphic expression, "one who urinates on a wall"—in Nabal's camp. Which is, as a matter of fact, what a strong force of cross-border raiders would have done had David not prevented it. In other words, "Nabal does not acknowledge that he has been protected? Let him find out what would have happened without protection."

David's vow is based on a standard form of vow found elsewhere, which goes like this: "God do to [my name], and more also, if I _____." We see this, for example, when David mourns over the death of Abner: "All the people came to urge David to eat bread while it was yet day; but David swore, saying, 'God do so to me, and more also, if I taste bread, or anything else, until the sun goes down' " (2 Samuel 3:35).

In the standard form, the penalty for breaking the vow is that God will do even worse harm to the one making the vow if he or she fails to fulfill it. But notice that in David's vow to take revenge on Nabal, the penalty for breaking it falls on "the enemies of David," not on David himself. This may indicate a reluctance to carry out the raid on a fellow Israelite; after all, at this point David has already been anointed king. Nabal, for all his obnoxious behavior, would become one of David's subjects. It may also explain how Abigail has time to assemble all the food and intercept him before he can carry out his threat. If he had moved immediately and in haste, it's difficult to see how she could have accomplished her mission in the time available.

The language of the vow, the seeming tardiness of his advance—these possibly indicate that David feels it necessary to make an example of Nabal but is not eager to kill those who would become his subjects. Perhaps it reflects the shepherd's instincts concerning an unruly member of his flock. However, reluctant or not, David set out to lead four hundred angry men on a punitive raid. But he had not reckoned on Abigail.

"As she rode on her donkey, and came down by the covert of the mountain, that behold, David and his men came down toward her, and she met them. . . . When Abigail saw David, she hurried and got off of her donkey, and fell before David on her face, and bowed herself to the ground. She fell at his feet, and said, 'On me, my lord, on me be the blame! Please let your servant speak in your ears. Hear the words of your servant. Please don't let my lord pay attention to this worthless fellow, Nabal; for as his name is, so is he. Nabal is his name, and folly is with him; but I, your servant, didn't see my lord's young men, whom you sent' " (1 Samuel 25:20, 23–25, WEB).

This sequence of events continues to follow the pattern of Jacob's entreaty of Esau. Abigail "falls on her face," that is, she kneels before David, touching her forehead to the ground. She follows this with a somewhat twisted argument. "Let the blame fall on me; hear my plea; ignore my worthless husband; I didn't see your messengers." So, "Blame me, but it's not my fault."

No doubt the food she had sent ahead, along with her attitude and her characterization of her husband as a "worthless fellow," which resonated with David's experience of the man, and not least her "beautiful face," had a positive effect. But all these are arguments that any woman might have used for self-preservation. It is the next part of Abigail's extended speech that raises her appeal to a much higher level. Instead of simply pleading for herself and her household, she appeals to David's highest aspirations.

"Now therefore, my lord, as Yahweh lives, and as your soul lives, since Yahweh has withheld you from blood guiltiness, and from avenging yourself with your own hand, now therefore let your enemies, and those who seek evil to my lord, be as Nabal" (verse 26, WEB).

Her subtle appeal testifies to her wisdom. It is Yahweh, she suggests, who has prevented David from murder. It's a fascinating anticipation of David's repentance after the murder of Uriah the Hittite, where he says, in Psalm 51:14 (WEB), "Deliver me from the guilt of bloodshed, O God, the God of my salvation." In fact, the whole Abigail narrative stands in contrast to the early Bathsheba encounter—but more about that later.

She now follows with subtle references to God's past guidance—"He will sling out your enemies' souls"—and to a future as king without the death of any of his subjects besmirching his reputation.

> "Now this present which your servant has brought to my lord, let it be given to the young men who follow my lord. Please forgive the trespass of your servant. For Yahweh will certainly make my lord a sure house, because my lord fights Yahweh's battles. Evil will not be found in you all your days.
> "Though men may rise up to pursue you, and to seek your soul, yet the soul of my lord will be bound in the bundle of life with Yahweh your God. He will sling out the souls of your enemies, as from the hollow of a sling.
> "It will come to pass, when Yahweh has done to my lord according to all the good that he has spoken concerning you, and has appointed you prince over Israel, that this shall be no grief to you, nor offense of heart to my lord, either that you have shed blood without cause, or that my lord has avenged himself. When Yahweh has dealt well with my lord, then remember your servant" (1 Samuel 25:27–31, WEB).

This soaring, prophetic speech envisions David at his greatest, not only as a successful soldier but as a compassionate sovereign and founder of a great dynasty. It is to this bright future that Abigail appeals, and it is this that elevates Abigail above just another wise woman. She lays out before David a vision of what, through God's grace, he might become, and appeals to him not to mar that bright future through an act of violence provoked by a fool. These inspiring words lift David's mood and his thoughts.

"David said to Abigail, 'Blessed is Yahweh, the God of Israel, who sent you today to meet me! Blessed is your discretion, and blessed are you, who have kept me today from blood guiltiness, and from avenging myself with my own hand. For indeed, as Yahweh, the God of Israel, lives, who has withheld me from harming you, unless you had hurried and come to meet me, surely there wouldn't have been left to Nabal by the morning light so much as one who urinates on a wall' " (verses 32–34, WEB).

David explicitly acknowledges that her counsel has prevented him from taking an action he would have regretted, and that her wisdom comes from God. By having him repeat to her verbatim what he had threatened to do, the author wants to impress upon the reader that this threat was real and came very close to being carried out, but for the intervention of Abigail.

Then David assures her that he will take no further action against her husband and sends her home. Nabal and his servants would surely have fallen to the swords of the raiding party, but Abigail with her soaring words and nourishing offerings had turned away David's anger. When she arrives back at camp, Nabal is in the midst of a shearing celebration, oblivious to the mortal danger from which Abigail has spared him. In another demonstration of her abiding wisdom, Abigail, seeing Nabal is "very drunk," says nothing to him; he will not remember it anyway, and in a drunken rage might make matters worse.

"In the morning, when the wine had gone out of Nabal, his wife told him these things, and his heart died within him, and he became as a stone. About ten days later, Yahweh struck Nabal, so that he died" (verses 37, 38, WEB).

The author portrayed Nabal as almost a comic figure, so foolish and clueless is he. When he sobers up and discovers how close he had come to death, the fear paralyzes him to the point that he dies ten days later.

Lest we miss the point of all this, the author has David sum up the action:

"When David heard that Nabal was dead, he said, 'Blessed is Yahweh, who has pleaded the cause of my reproach from the hand of Nabal, and has kept back his servant from evil. Yahweh has returned the evildoing of Nabal on his own head' " (verse 39, WEB).

David will be king. Abigail not only reminded him of that, but she helped him become more kingly, to act as a magnanimous sovereign, not merely an ambitious warlord. Recognizing her wisdom, David decides he needs such a woman as his queen.

"David sent and spoke concerning Abigail, to take her to himself as wife. When David's servants had come to Abigail to Carmel, they spoke to her, saying, 'David has sent us to you, to take you to him as wife' " (verses 39, 40).

Abigail quickly complies. David previously had a wife, Michal, the daughter of King Saul. David acquired Michal as a connection to Saul's royal house, but her presence continually served to emphasize his distance from Saul, rather than his connection. And as a final insult to David, Saul gave her as wife to someone else. Michal, born a princess, does not exhibit nobility of behavior or of character. She does not act like true royalty, nor does she bring out nobility in anyone near her.

What a contrast is Abigail, a woman trapped in a bad marriage, endangered by her foolish first husband, threatened by proud men and their angry words; yet, seizing her opportunity, she saves a future king from folly, sets him on a path to becoming a better man and monarch, and eventually becomes his queen.

David may be a "man after God's own heart," but throughout his life he will listen to only a few individuals. Abigail, at this critical juncture, is one of them. She supplies the wise counsel David needs.

In this episode Abigail serves as David's "strong partner," providing what he needs to make him more regal, more noble, more worthy to be king. Had he included her more in his life, he might have avoided some of the serious mistakes that later marred his reign. Sadly for David, Abigail is mentioned only in passing after this episode. Perhaps he had spent too many hours alone with the sheep as a youth, but David apparently did not forge healthy relationships with people. And so he failed to let Abigail fulfill the role that such a wise queen might have had. But that is David's doing, not Abigail's.

Spiritually, Abigail could be a match for either Samuel or Nathan, the two prophets whom David relied on. The rabbis consider her a prophet, and one of the Seven Great Beauties in the Bible. Two of David's wives, Michal and Bathsheba, raised serious questions because of their actions. Of other wives, such as Ahinoam, for example, we know very little. Among all the women in David's life, only Abigail has nothing evil reported about her, and what we do know highlights her wisdom, humility, and beauty—both of appearance and character.

Throughout the Old Testament, these stories of women who took the lead have been from different periods in Israel's history. With Abigail and our next woman, Bathsheba, we encounter two women whose stories and destinies are forever tied with that of David—and with each other.

NINE

BATHSHEBA
WIFE OF DAVID, MOTHER OF SOLOMON

Bathsheba. The name brings with it a tangled web of lust, infidelity, intrigue, treachery, and murder. She has been portrayed as a seductress, flaunting her nakedness before the king, eagerly seeking a place at the palace, and alternatively as an innocent wife, going about her own business, with no choice but to obey the royal summons. Frankly, the biblical narrative about the adultery focuses almost exclusively on David's actions, so that it gives no indication of her thoughts or motivations. She bathed, he saw, he summoned, she came to the palace. When she became pregnant as a result, David sent her home and sent to the battlefield for her husband to return to his home, so as to cloud the issue of paternity. When that failed, he conspired with Joab to have Uriah killed in battle.

The story represents a soldier's worst fear. The king takes advantage of his absence by seducing the soldier's wife, and then he arranges for the soldier to be killed in battle. It is the lowest form of treachery for a king, a betrayal of the basest sort. This narrative exposes the depth of David's depravity for all to see. On the other hand, this same biblical author, so skilled at using just the right verb to indicate attitude, and the precise words of dialogue to hint at motive, does none of that concerning Bathsheba. During all this drama, the narrative portrays Bathsheba as a physical beauty but an otherwise blank character, speaking only these words: "I'm pregnant."

To portray her as a temptress attributes motives and actions far too elaborate and detailed to resemble the actual woman sketched in the text. In fact, the entire narrative of her early encounter with King David can be boiled down to "beautiful, compliant, pregnant."

However, Bathsheba did not make the list in this book because of the initial episode. She shows no initiative, almost no will at all in it. Four decades later, however, she plays a crucial role.

David lay dying. Never before in Israel's history had a king died of natural causes and without an anointed successor. Adonijah, David's fourth son (his older brothers, Amnon and Absalom, being dead), decided to seize the opportunity.

"Then Adonijah the son of Haggith exalted himself, saying, 'I will be king.' Then he prepared him chariots and horsemen, and fifty men to run before him. . . . He conferred with Joab the son of Zeruiah, and with Abiathar the priest; and they followed Adonijah and helped him" (1 Kings 1:5, 7, WEB).

Adonijah shrewdly assumes the mantle of heir apparent, consolidating his claim by enlisting the support of Abiathar the priest, and Joab, David's chief general. Joab had proved himself both loyal and ruthless. Loyal because he conspired with David in the death of Uriah the Hittite without raising any objection, and ruthless in the revenge killing of Abner, and what was essentially an execution of Absalom, despite David's orders not to harm his son.

However, not everyone supported Adonijah's claim. "But Zadok the priest, Benaiah the son of Jehoiada, Nathan the prophet, Shimei, Rei, and the mighty men who belonged to David, were not with Adonijah" (verse 8, WEB).

Zadok, Nathan, and the rest represent a powerful group of men, but they lack one thing—a credible person to take the throne. A monarchy needs a monarch. No matter your influence, if you lacked a prospective king, your opposition would mean little. Meanwhile, Adonijah moves swiftly to consolidate his claim. He prepares a feast to celebrate his accession to the throne.

"Adonijah killed sheep, cattle, and fatlings by the stone of Zoheleth, which is beside En Rogel; and he called all his brothers, the king's sons, and all the men of Judah, the king's servants; but he didn't call Nathan the prophet, and Benaiah, and the mighty men, and Solomon his brother" (1 Kings 1:9, 10, WEB).

Note who is included in the guest list and who is excluded. Adonijah invites all of his supporters and none who oppose him. There will be no dissent over his claim to the throne at this celebration. Most notable, of course, is the absence of Solomon, his rival. Unspoken is the mortal threat; it was common in that culture for the new king to exterminate his rivals and his enemies.

"Then Nathan spoke to Bathsheba the mother of Solomon, saying, 'Haven't you heard that Adonijah the son of Haggith reigns, and David our lord doesn't know it? Now therefore come, please let me give you counsel, that you may save your own life, and your son Solomon's life. Go in to king David, and tell him, "Didn't you, my lord, king, swear to your servant, saying, 'Assuredly Solomon your son shall reign after me, and he shall sit on my throne?' Why then does Adonijah reign?" Behold, while you are still talking there with the king, I will also come in after you and confirm your words' " (1 Kings 1:11-14, WEB).

Nathan gives voice to the unspoken threat. Bathsheba needs to act to save her life, and Solomon's life. Nathan is the recognized prophet, and he will back her up. But Nathan realizes that Bathsheba wields an influence over David that only a beloved wife can.

She and Nathan carry out their plan, and David responds by officially proclaiming Solomon as his successor. That settles the issue, and Solomon begins what will be the last reign of a united Israel.

It's easy to minimize Bathsheba's role here. But imagine what would have happened had she failed to act.

The history of Israel is unimaginable without the reign of Solomon. Solomon the wise, Solomon who built the temple. Solomon represents the "golden age" of the monarchy. Bathsheba not only gave birth to Solomon, the man; in a real sense she gave birth to Solomon the king. Compared to some of the other women in Scripture, her role is rather small. But small does not mean insignificant. And there are two more reasons to include her in this list of women who took the lead.

Of all the Old Testament women whose stories we include, only two stories are linked to each other: Abigail and Bathsheba. The important influence these two women wield in the reign of David—the most important of the Israelite monarchs—means their stories are forever linked with his, and with each other.

Both of the women are wives of David. Each of them is a crucial figure, although at the opposite ends of his reign. David encounters and weds Abigail before he becomes king. He marries Bathsheba while king, but more important, through the accession of Solomon, Bathsheba's influence continues after his reign. Indeed, as we examine David's interactions with these two women, we see how Bathsheba serves as a mirror to Abigail in two very different ways.

Abigail	**Bathsheba—Early**	**Bathsheba—Late**
Meets David before reign	Meets David during reign	Influences David at the end of his reign
Prevents him from killing a future subject and marring his reign	Is the reason he conspires to kill a valiant soldier, marring his reign	Prevents the assassination of Solomon
Inspires regal behavior	Inspires treacherous behavior	Ensures regal legacy

As the table demonstrates, the early Bathsheba influences David—whether intentional or not—in the opposite way to Abigail, while the late Bathsheba influences David in the same, positive way Abigail had. Saying that the early Bathsheba influenced David in a negative way does not indicate an evaluation of her personally, but rather the effect she had on his actions. As mentioned earlier, the narrative focuses on David almost exclusively, so we have no way of knowing whether she approved or disapproved of his actions. By contrast, she clearly participated in a positive way at the end of his life.

Finally, Bathsheba had to be included, because Matthew includes her in Jesus' genealogy. And with the inclusion of her story, we can now examine why Matthew listed the four women he did.

We have already noted that all four of the women—Tamar, Rahab, Ruth, and Bathsheba—have questionable connections. So why highlight them in Jesus' genealogy?

I believe there were two reasons: first, because of the fifth woman.

"Jacob became the father of Joseph, the husband of Mary, from whom was born Jesus" (Matthew 1:16, WEB).

Both Matthew and Luke affirm that Mary conceived Jesus by the Holy Spirit, that she became pregnant *before* she married Joseph. Take this story out of the New Testament, put it into everyday experience, and you get something like this:

A young woman becomes pregnant before marriage; both she and her groom-to-be affirm that they had not yet had sex when this happened; the girl claims the infant is a child of the Holy Spirit.

Let's be honest. This looks like a tabloid headline story: "Girl claims God made her pregnant, not fiancé."

It is inevitable that questions about the child's legitimacy—and Matthew makes it clear, these questions occurred to Joseph himself—would arise. Rumors might well follow the child His whole life. It is possible that John records the expression of such doubts in his Gospel. "They said to him, 'We were not born of sexual immorality'" (John 8:41, WEB).

Origen, one of the early church fathers, considered this to be an effort to discredit Jesus by alluding to rumors of His being illegitimate. For some, especially some Jews, even a hint of scandal, an appearance of impropriety, would be enough to disqualify Jesus from being the Messiah.

Matthew was a Jew, and he knew of this mind-set. He had no doubts about Jesus' birth, as his account demonstrates. But the questions could not simply be ignored; they would not go away, even if denied. Matthew wanted to break through the prejudice of those inclined to write Jesus off because of questions concerning His birth. And that's what the mention of these other four women does. If they, with their questionable connections, could be included as ancestors of kings, then so could Mary. Even the worst interpretation of her pregnancy—that she conceived as a result of fornication—would not make her a prostitute, as Rahab was and Tamar pretended to be. She was not a Gentile, as all of them but Bathsheba were. Nor had she committed adultery, as Bathsheba had.

Matthew believed that Mary had conceived by the Holy Spirit, but his first concern was to establish that Jesus was the Messiah, the King/Deliverer. Once people believed Jesus to be the Deliverer, they then might come to believe in the virgin birth. But first they might need to overcome questions about his mother's reputation. The four women listed earlier in the genealogy clear up that question decisively. Undeniably, God uses flawed human beings to accomplish His will.

Although Matthew wrote his Gospel specifically for the Jews, he also realized that Jesus came to deliver all mankind. And that, I believe, is the second reason for including the four questionable women. Three of them are Gentiles, and the fourth was the wife of a Gentile, Uriah the Hittite. If Gentiles can be part of the lineage of the Messiah, then surely they can be recipients of His deliverance from sin. Matthew ends his account, you remember, with the gospel going into all the world. There are hints throughout his Gospel that this will happen, beginning, I believe, with the four women in the genealogy.

Bathsheba is the last of these four, a foundational figure in Israel's history. Wife of David, mother of Solomon—the two greatest kings of Israel. As mentioned earlier, very few seem able to counsel with David. He listened to Samuel while he was alive, and to Nathan; then at crucial junctures he listened to Abigail and Bathsheba. God meets people where they are, and it's no use speculating which one woman should have been David's wife. Suffice to say that Abigail and Bathsheba combined, at opposite ends of David's reign, to be the strong partner he desperately needed.

In many of the Psalms we see David's strong emotions that led him to a deep relationship with God, but which also sometimes led him astray. It is ironic, then, that it was a woman—when women are commonly stereotyped as emotional—who would aid him in making the sober-minded, sensible choice at crucial points in his life. Without Bathsheba, David would not have been the David we know; there would have been no Solomon, and later, no Solomon as king.

TEN

WOMAN OF SHUNEM
GENEROSITY REPAID

Now the king was talking with Gehazi the servant of the man of God, saying, 'Please tell me all the great things that Elisha has done'" (2 Kings 8:4, WEB).

Sometimes two stories intertwine so closely that it is impossible to tell one without telling the other. We think of Romeo and Juliet, Damon and Pythias, Antony and Cleopatra. In the Bible, we have Cain and Abel, Jacob and Esau, David and Saul, Elijah and Jezebel, among others. As Gehazi is about to demonstrate, it is impossible to tell of the "great things that Elisha has done" without mentioning the Woman of Shunem. Make no mistake: Elisha did many great things. Only Jesus Himself, in all of Scripture, performed more miracles than Elisha. And as Gehazi recognized, the Woman of Shunem occupied a central, though subdued, role in Elisha's ministry.

Two of his greatest miracles would not have taken place but for the perception, initiative, and persistent hospitality of the Woman of Shunem.

"One day Elisha went to Shunem, where there was a prominent woman; and she persuaded him to eat bread. So it was, that as often as he passed by, he turned in there to eat bread. She said to her husband, 'See now, I perceive that this is a holy man of God who passes by us continually. Please let us make a little room on the roof. Let us set for him there a bed, a table, a chair, and a lamp stand. When he comes to us, he can stay there'" (2 Kings 4:8–10, WEB).

Early in his ministry Elisha encountered this "prominent woman," the Woman of Shunem. We are not told what made her prominent, although subsequent events reveal that her husband must have been a man of significant property. But this woman would have been prominent, even if penniless, for she demonstrated insight, initiative, and hospitality. She persuaded Elisha to dine in her home. Not only that, but she encouraged him to stop and eat with her and her husband whenever he passed through Shunem.

She tells her husband that she perceives Elisha to be a "holy man of God." Recognizing that God is blessing Israel through Elisha, she wants to support that work fully. Not content with merely providing food, she persuades her husband to construct a small apartment with all the amenities, just for Elisha. As anyone knows who travels the same route repeatedly, having such a haven is a great blessing. And we recognize that quiet souls like the Woman of Shunem are constantly at work in the background, easing the burdens and lightening the load of those, like Elisha, whose ministry is much more visible. But those quiet souls are as much a part of the miracles as the prophet who performs them.

"One day he [Elisha] came there, and he went to the room and lay there. He said to Gehazi his servant, 'Call this Shunammite.' When he had called her, she stood before him. He said to him, 'Say now to her, "Behold, you have cared for us with all this care. What is to be done for you? Would you like to be spoken for to the king, or to the captain of the army?" ' She answered, 'I dwell among my own people' " (verses 11–13, WEB).

One day, as he relaxes in his private apartment, Elisha, recognizing the great blessings this woman has provided, decides the time has come to recognize and reward her. A tiny village, distant from the capital of Samaria or any fortified city, Elisha offers to use his influence with the king, or the royal army, on her behalf. Content with her lot, living among people she knows and trusts, she has neither the need nor ambition for royal attention. In Elisha's day, just as in our own, those who give—truly give—with no strings attached are rare jewels. The Woman of Shunem proves herself to be one.

Ralph Waldo Emerson said, "You cannot give anything to a magnanimous person. After you have served him, he at once puts you in debt by his magnanimity." The Woman of Shunem embodies Emerson's statement. At her own initiative, she has provided Elisha with food, shelter, and rest—and even more important, with hospitality. One can purchase food, shelter, a bed, but hospitality, making one feel comfortable when not at home, is a gift. And when Elisha suggests possible compensation, she demurs. She does not need or desire what he offers. But God can provide what man cannot.

"He [Elijah] said, 'What then is to be done for her?' Gehazi answered, 'Most certainly she has no son, and her husband is old' " (verse 14, WEB).

"She has no son, and her husband is old." By now we recognize the circumstance as a familiar one: the Barren Woman, but as always, with a twist. As with all the other barren women, wealthy or not, uncertainty clouds this woman's future. Without a son, but with an aging husband, she soon will be without human support. Even with wealth, her situation remains somewhat precarious—as we shall soon see.

Such realities might have made a lesser person self-focused. But in the Woman of Shunem we see no insecurity, no anxiety for self-preservation. And that is the twist. Tamar and Hannah both pursued—in different ways—their strong desire for a son. But if the Woman of Shunem longs for a son, we have not seen the slightest indication of that longing. On the contrary, she declares herself to be content. Apparently, she has made peace with her status.

"He said, 'Call her.' When he had called her, she stood in the door. He said, 'At this season, when the time comes around, you will embrace a son.' She said, 'No, my lord, you man of God, do not lie to your servant' " (verses 15, 16, WEB).

"Do not lie to me" sounds somewhat harsh to our ears. It is important to remember that biblical Hebrew consists of only a few thousand words, and so there are few choices. We might say, "Are you serious?" or "Don't tease me like that!" and express approximately the same thing: amazement and reluctance to be disappointed so deeply. Contented she may have been, yet her words reveal how great a blessing she perceives this to be. Apparently, with her husband aging, she thought it beyond possibility for her to have a son. Even though she had not expressed the least concern about being childless, this promise of Elisha's reveals her inner desire.

True to the prophet's word, "the woman conceived, and bore a son at that season, when the time came around, as Elisha had said to her" (verse 17, WEB).

But life was harsh in those days, and death lurked in every circumstance. Tragically, it struck this son of promise. "When the child was grown, one day he went out to his father to the reapers. He said to his father, 'My head! My head!' He said to his servant, 'Carry him to his mother.' When he had taken him, and brought him to his mother, he sat on her knees until noon, and then died" (verses 18–20, WEB).

Enough time has passed so that the boy reaches the age when he can accompany his father into the fields at harvest, but he's still young enough to get carried away in the excitement of the event and forget about his own needs. Harvest, of course, best takes place on a sunny day. In fact, most grains cannot be harvested when the plants are wet. Sometime during the day, the boy begins to experience a headache, not uncommon for one who has become overheated. One of the servants carries the boy home to his mother, who cares for him. But around midday he dies in her arms.

Few experiences devastate one so much as losing a child. We would expect the mother to be hysterical with grief. But not the Woman of Shunem. Yet again, she behaves in an extraordinary way.

"She went up and laid him on the man of God's bed, and shut the door on him, and went out. She called to her husband, and said, 'Please send me one of the servants, and one of the donkeys, that I may run to the man of God, and come again.' He said, 'Why would you want go to him today? It is not a new moon or a Sabbath.' She said, 'It's [all] right' " (verses 21–23, WEB).

We can but wonder at this woman's seemingly calm demeanor. Her only son has just died, and her actions appear orderly, even businesslike. Clearly she has a plan. First, she places the boy on Elisha's bed and shuts the door. We are not told why. Then she calls to her husband, requesting a servant and a donkey, so that she "may run to the man of God, and come again."

Puzzled, her husband notes that it is neither a new moon nor a Sabbath. Given that she has a lengthy journey in view—she wants a donkey—in this case the Sabbath mentioned is not *the* Sabbath. New moons and certain other days were considered sabbaths, that is, feast days. Given her habit of hospitality, she probably often invited Elisha to their home for such celebrations. But this is not one of those days, as the husband mentions; it is neither a new moon nor a Sabbath.

Her reply, "It's all right," is amazing under the circumstances. Her prophetically promised only son has just died, and it's *all right?* How can she make such a calm reply? We have already seen, when asked what Elisha can do for her, that the Woman of Shunem possesses an exceptionally practical nature. Surely that comes into play here. But I think there may be two more reasons.

First, Gehazi told Elisha that her husband was old nearly a year before the child was born. Several years have passed since the boy's birth, so the father has aged as well. It may well be that the Woman of Shunem fears that if she tells the aging man that his only son and heir has died, the shock and grief might do him in. The fact that she shut the door on the room where the child's body lay may indicate that she does not want the father to discover the child's fate. Second, I believe that she has steadfast faith: God gave her the child, and He will not let the child be taken from her so soon. Her plan—to go see Elisha—and her subsequent actions carrying out that plan demonstrate that faith.

"Then she saddled a donkey, and said to her servant, 'Drive, and go forward! Don't slow down for me, unless I ask you to' " (verse 24, WEB).

Exactly what she wants the servant to "drive" is unclear. But her words leave no doubt that she wants to go to the prophet with all haste—as fast as she can take it.

"So she went, and came to the man of God to Mount Carmel. When the man of God saw her afar off, he said to Gehazi his servant, 'Behold, there is the Shunammite. Please run now to meet her, and ask her, "Is it well with you? Is it well with your husband? Is it well with your child?" ' " (verses 25, 26, WEB).

Elisha sees the woman at some distance, no doubt because he is at a high elevation (Mount Carmel). He probably makes the same calculation her husband did: *This is not a new moon or a Sabbath,* he thinks. *Why is she coming to me today, and in such haste?* Alarmed, he sends his servant on the run to meet her and inquire about the welfare of herself and her family.

"She answered, 'It is well' " (verse 26, WEB).

Once again came the strangely calm answer. Perhaps it expresses her strong faith; perhaps she simply refuses to discuss her situation with anyone but the prophet. When she finally reaches him, her aspect changes dramatically.

"When she came to the man of God to the hill, she caught hold of his feet. Gehazi came near to thrust her away; but the man of God said, 'Leave her alone; for her soul is troubled within her; and Yahweh has hidden it from me, and has not told me' " (verse 27, WEB).

These few words contain so many fascinating details. This woman, who has avoided all overt signs of grief, suddenly becomes the picture of sorrow, all the more so because she says nothing, makes no sound at all, but throws herself prone at Elisha's feet.

In Gehazi's attempt to "thrust her away," we see the faithful protector. Although not mentioned directly, Elisha must have constantly been the object of urgent petitioners eager to command his attention, to seek his favor and his actions on their behalf. Gehazi's actions demonstrate his concern for his master, not insensitivity to the woman.

And then there's the puzzlement of Elisha. He sees the woman is distraught but does not know why. God has not shown him, and this surprises him. But he recognizes that the Woman of Shunem, so practical, so unemotional, is experiencing tremendous emotional distress, and he wants to know why.

> Then she said, "Did I ask you for a son, my lord? Didn't I say, 'Do not deceive me'?"
> Then he said to Gehazi, "Tuck your cloak into your belt, take my staff in your hand, and go your way. If you meet any man, don't greet him; and if anyone greets you, don't answer him again. Then lay my staff on the child's face" (verses 28, 29, WEB).

The woman's appeal sounds strange to our ears—"Did I ask you for a son? Didn't I say, 'Do not deceive me'?" The best I can make of it is something like this: "I didn't ask you for this child; I was content. But once you gave him to me, it is unfair to let me think I could really experience a joy I had become resigned to live without, and then take him from me in an untimely fashion." If she was like almost any woman, it had taken fortitude and great faith to resign herself to being childless. But to have a child given to her after that struggle, only to have him taken away—it was more than she could bear.

Elisha recognizes that only acute illness or death itself could have moved this woman to act as she had. So he tells his servant to run as fast as he can, letting nothing delay him, and lay the prophet's staff on the child's face.

There is an interesting sidelight here. The words "Tuck your cloak into your belt" are a clearer translation of the more literal "gird up your loins," which we find in several places in Scripture. Doing this allows the wearer to stride and maneuver more freely, and run faster. And that is the point of all this. Gehazi is to go as fast as he can.

"The child's mother said, 'As Yahweh lives, and as your soul lives, I will not leave you.' So he arose, and followed her" (verse 30, WEB).

By now we are no longer surprised by this woman's tenacity. She vows not to leave the prophet, and he believes her. It's as though she's saying, "This is all your doing; it's up to you to take care of it." And, as his actions demonstrate, Elisha agrees with her. He asked God to give this woman a son as a blessing and aid in her old age. Unless something dramatic takes place, that will not now happen.

On the way to Shunem, Gehazi returns with solemn tidings:

"Gehazi went ahead of them, and laid the staff on the child's face; but there was no voice or hearing. Therefore he returned to meet him, and told him, 'The child has not awakened' " (verse 31, WEB).

At this point, there can be no doubt that the woman's tenacity, her insistence that Elisha must deal with this crisis himself, is justified. Gehazi has faithfully followed the prophet's instructions, to no effect. What follows next is, well, unusual: "When Elisha had come into the house, behold, the child was dead, and lying on his bed. He went in therefore, and shut the door on them both, and prayed to Yahweh. He went up, and lay on the child, and put his mouth on his mouth, and his eyes on his eyes, and his hands on his hands. He stretched himself on him; and the child's flesh grew warm. Then he returned, and walked in the house once back and forth; and went up, and stretched himself out on him. Then the child sneezed seven times, and the child opened his eyes" (verses 32–35, WEB).

I would like to explain every detail of this extraordinary episode, but I cannot. I have read multiple explanations of the seven sneezes, most of them somewhat allegorical and none of them convincing. We do know that seven in the Bible is the number of maturity, of completion, even perfection. Exactly what the seven sneezes indicate here is not clear—except that they tell us the child has been revived. Corpses don't sneeze. And that is enough to know. Elisha, through the power of God, had brought this child of promise back to life.

"He called Gehazi, and said, 'Call this Shunammite!' So he called her. When she had come in to him, he said, 'Take up your son.' Then she went in, fell at his feet, and bowed herself to the ground; then she picked up her son, and went out" (verses 36, 37, WEB).

Accustomed as we are to the minimalist prose we often find in the Old Testament, this ending still seems unbelievably terse. The Woman of Shunem does not speak at all in these verses. She demonstrates her gratitude by her actions of reverence—falling at Elisha's feet, bowing to the ground—not with words. But we have seen that repeatedly. The woman lets her actions speak for her, and generally she uses only as many words as necessary to communicate. Her answers to questions have been short indeed:

"*I dwell among my own people.*"
"*It's all right.*"
"*It is well.*"

The last two answers were given just after her only son had died! Even when told she will miraculously have a child, she does not break out into song, as Hannah did. Instead, she guards against disappointment: "Did I ask you for a son? Don't lie to me!" And yet she is neither cold nor uncaring. Her concern for Elisha demonstrates that. If ever a woman broke the stereotype of females being overly emotional, the Woman of Shunem shatters it!

Still, the ending leaves the story feeling incomplete, unfinished. That's because it is.

"Now Elisha had spoken to the woman whose son he had restored to life, saying, 'Arise, and go, you and your household, and stay for a while wherever you can; for Yahweh has called for a famine. It will also come on the land for seven years' " (2 Kings 8:1, WEB).

Approximately two years pass. Elisha continues to watch over the Woman of Shunem. He warns her of a coming famine, telling her to go elsewhere to survive the disaster. Notice that the story does not mention her husband at all, except as he might be included in "your household." A number of years have passed since the son's birth, and her husband had been called old well before that. Perhaps he has died in the intervening years. Perhaps he has become ill and no longer has the strength to run things. In any case, clearly the Woman of Shunem now rules the household.

If a famine can be called fascinating, this one is. Elisha apparently told no one else about the coming famine, as we have no other mentions of it. We do not know precisely when this took place, again, for lack of other mention. It appears that Elisha singled out this woman and her household to warn them; her continuing ministry to his needs perhaps aroused a desire to care for her. And having first provided her with a son, and then restoring him, it seems Elisha determined not to let that be in vain. He saw to her and her son's continued survival.

The length of the famine, seven years in duration, stimulates interest for another reason. You may remember that on the day of his ascension by fiery chariot, Elijah inquired what gift Elisha desired from him:

"Elijah said to Elisha, 'Ask what I shall do for you, before I am taken from you.' Elisha said, 'Please let a double portion of your spirit be on me.' He said, 'You have asked a hard thing. If you see me when I am taken from you, it will be so for you; but if not, it will not be so' " (2 Kings 2:9, 10, WEB).

As we have mentioned several times, the "double portion" refers to the inheritance received by the firstborn. Since Elisha did see Elijah taken, he did receive that double portion. We also mentioned that no one in Scripture performed more miracles than Elisha, except for Jesus Himself. In sheer numbers, Elisha performed many more miracles than his predecessor. But here we find one place where a two-to-one ratio exists: the length of the two famines.

The drought brought on by Elijah's prayers lasted three and a half years. The famine mentioned in the story of the Woman of Shunem lasts precisely twice as long: seven years. We have seen that biblical authors only mention details that matter. And why the precise length of this famine—mentioned nowhere else—should matter is unclear, unless it pertains to the double portion.

"The woman arose, and did according to the man of God's word. She went with her household, and lived in the land of the Philistines for seven years. At the end of seven years, the woman returned from the land of the Philistines. Then she went out to beg the king for her house and for her land" (2 Kings 8:2, 3, WEB).

This is where we started this chapter. She returns to ask for her land, just as the king has asked Gehazi to tell him of all the great things Elisha has done.

"As he was telling the king how he had restored to life him who was dead, behold, the woman, whose son he had restored to life, begged the king for her house and for her land. Gehazi said, 'My lord, O king, this is the woman, and this is her son, whom Elisha restored to life.' When the king asked the woman, she told him. So the king appointed to her a certain officer, saying, 'Restore all that was hers, and all the fruits of the field since the day that she left the land, even until now' " (verses 5, 6, WEB).

We have now come full circle—Elisha had first offered to speak to the king, or the captain of the army, on her behalf, but the Woman of Shunem had replied, "I dwell among my own people." Now, after seven years of not dwelling among her own people, but among the Philistines, she comes before the king with a request. But she does not come anonymously. Gehazi identifies her as the woman whose son Elisha had raised from the dead. So, in the person of his servant, Gehazi, Elisha has fulfilled his first offer, speaking to the king on her behalf.

The king orders not only that her land but also all the "fruits," that is, all the crops that would have been harvested in those seven years from that land, be restored to her. Probably, in her absence, and during a famine, her land had reverted to possession of the king. Even today, that is what happens to unclaimed property. Restoring her land would have been a boon. But restoring to her what the land had produced, whether in actual commodities such as grain or in value with coin, represented an act of great generosity.

The preacher tells us: "Cast your bread on the waters; for you shall find it after many days" (Ecclesiastes 11:1, WEB).

And later Jesus would tell us: "Give, and it will be given to you: good measure, pressed down, shaken together, and running over, will be given to you" (Luke 6:38, WEB).

Surely the Woman of Shunem experienced that. She sees a need for Elisha to have a place of solitude and rest and helps provide it. We know she has no ulterior motive, for when Elisha offers to do something for her, she claims to need nothing. But through the power of God, Elisha gives her something she could only dream of—a son. When that son tragically died, Elisha raised him from the dead. He protected her from famine by warning her to flee. And at least partially due to his influence, her land and all that she might have gained through seven years was restored to her. Truly her generosity came back to her.

But there is more to this woman than generosity. She demonstrated practical wisdom, foreseeing Elisha's needs; great faith, for even in the face of tragedy, she never gave way to grief or fear; and level-headedness, even in the face of crisis.

As we said in the beginning, the story of Elisha and his ministry is inextricably intertwined with the story of the Woman of Shunem. Although she is married to another, and Elisha never married, as far as we know, spiritually and in ministry they are each other's strong partners. The Woman of Shunem not only facilitates Elisha's journeys and ministry, but she herself is the object of several of his greatest miracles. Remove her story and the ministry of Elisha would be greatly diminished.

ELEVEN

Esther
The Girl They Left Behind

"Don't think to yourself that you will escape . . ." The words stung the young queen, the most recent shock in a series of frightening events. As she looked around her at the opulent furnishings, the elegant clothing, servants to tend to her every whim—yet once again she felt herself alone, the orphan girl who had been left behind.

Yes, Hadasseh and her older cousin, Mordecai, were left behind. That's not the way we see it, because we know the end of the story, but that was what they went through. The "good" Jews had left Persia following three separate calls to leave their exile—that's right, three calls to "come out of 'Babylon.'" Thousands of Jews returned to Judea and Jerusalem. Those who remained may have been looked upon as less devout, even less Jewish, and they may well have felt left out or left behind. But could it possibly have been the right decision for them? After all, Mordecai—so far as we know, a single man—had Hadasseh to think about.

Looking back, she could see the challenges her uncle faced. If he returned to Jerusalem, how could he, a single man, care for an orphan girl, make a living, help construct the walls, and bear arms at all times, as men had to do in the hostile environment that surrounded Jerusalem for years during its rebuilding? Whatever regrets Mordecai may have had, Haddasseh, now called Esther, believed he had made the right choice by remaining in Susa. He had a good job in the royal bureaucracy, even if some of his Jewish friends thought him somewhat disloyal to his people and less faithful to God for doing so. After all, the prophet Daniel had served kings who sometimes did evil things.

Mordecai surely had his critics. Some of his Jewish detractors might have asked if he fancied himself as a Daniel. Of course, he did not. But if Daniel had been right to serve pagan rulers in large matters, why couldn't Mordecai serve such leaders in small ways? So the two remained in exile, and Mordecai cared for his cousin and protected her until she grew into a young woman. And then came the series of events that changed her life forever.

It began with Queen Vashti's defiance and then her banishment, the news of which spread throughout the Persian Empire.

> "Therefore, if it pleases the king, let him issue a royal decree and let it be written in the laws of Persia and Media, which cannot be repealed, that Vashti is never again to enter the presence of King Xerxes. Also let the king give her royal position to someone else who is better than she. Then when the king's edict is proclaimed throughout all his vast realm, all the women will respect their husbands, from the least to the greatest."
>
> The king and his nobles were pleased with this advice, so the king did as Memukan proposed. He sent dispatches to all parts of the kingdom, to each province in its own script and to each people in their own language, proclaiming that every man should be ruler over his own household, using his native tongue (Esther 1:19–22).

It is difficult not to be amused at these powerful men, afraid that their wives will rise up in rebellion because of a single act of disobedience on the part of the queen. And one has to wonder how wise it was to send out a proclamation that, in effect, broadcasts the queen's mini-rebellion. Imagine an elementary teacher telling a new class all the mischief they should *not* commit; it ends up giving them ideas of misbehavior that they wouldn't have come up with on their own. Foolish or not, that's what they did.

The maiden was fair...

With the position of queen open, and at the advice of these same tremulous wise men, Xerxes sent messengers to scour the land for beautiful young women to fill the office Vashti had vacated. Hadasseh was beautiful, and so she was summoned to the palace to prepare for her audience with the king.

> "This young woman, who was also known as Esther, had a lovely figure and was beautiful.... When the king's order and edict had been proclaimed, many young women were brought to the citadel of Susa and put under the care of Hegai. Esther also was taken to the king's palace.... Esther had not revealed her nationality and family background, because Mordecai had forbidden her to do so" (Esther 2:7, 8, 10).

When or why Haddasseh changed her name, we are not told, but she arrived at the palace in Susa as Esther. Perhaps it was part of the concealment of her ethnicity. It may be that Mordecai and Esther no longer lived as observant Jews. The name Mordecai, after all, is a form of Marduk, the name of Babylon's great god. The Persian Empire was an ancient rarity, for it did not equate religion and state. The Persians allowed freedom of religion. Babylon is an example of empires that did not. When the Babylonians conquered a nation, they believed that their war god, Marduk, had conquered the other nation's god.

In any case, no one knew precisely what it meant to live as a Jew in exile without an available temple for sacrifice or feast days. God had condemned Jeroboam for setting up a place of worship other than in Jerusalem, complicating the whole matter. This provided another reason why so many faithful Jews returned to Jerusalem, and why those who did not were considered perhaps not as righteous. In this case, it seems fair to say that prudence dictated that Mordecai and his young charge remain in Susa.

"Esther . . . was taken to the king's palace and entrusted to Hegai, who had charge of the harem. She pleased him and won his favor. Immediately he provided her with her beauty treatments and special food. He assigned to her seven female attendants selected from the king's palace and moved her and her attendants into the best place in the harem" (verses 8, 9).

We often hear that beauty is skin deep, but that is inaccurate. Prettiness is skin deep. True beauty radiates from the inmost being and thence out through the skin. Hegai's treatment of Esther identifies her as a true beauty. The man—a eunuch—is the master of the king's harem, surrounded by physically attractive women. Yet Hegai "immediately" gives Esther cosmetics and provisions and ladies in waiting, and the best place in the harem, because she pleases him. In that population of pretty girls and women, it must have been Esther's beauty of demeanor and character that set her apart. And the narrative will soon verify her winsome character.

"Every day he [Mordecai] walked back and forth near the courtyard of the harem to find out how Esther was and what was happening to her" (verse 11).

We recognize this scene. The concerned father figure, continually patrolling near where the young woman lives, to see that—insofar as he can do anything—she prospers.

"Before a young woman's turn came to go in to King Xerxes . . . this is how she would go to the king: Anything she wanted was given her to take with her from the harem to the king's palace. . . . When the turn came for Esther (the young woman Mordecai had adopted, the daughter of his uncle Abihail) to go to the king, she asked for nothing other than what Hegai, the king's eunuch who was in charge of the harem, suggested. And Esther won the favor of everyone who saw her" (verses 12, 13, 15).

Here we see more evidence of Esther's intelligence and humility, which together produce wisdom. When her turn comes to see the king, she seeks and follows the counsel of Hegai. It has been his job for years to help please the king, and she avails herself of his experience and knowledge. Many a pretty girl, accustomed to deference, thinks she knows more than those around her. Not Esther—she is ready to learn. And she charms Xerxes as well.

"Now the king was attracted to Esther more than to any of the other women, and she won his favor and approval more than any of the other virgins. So he set a royal crown on her head and made her queen instead of Vashti. And the king gave a great banquet, Esther's banquet, for all his nobles and officials. He proclaimed a holiday throughout the provinces and distributed gifts with royal liberality" (verses 17, 18).

In an interesting irony, Xerxes makes a feast to celebrate Esther's elevation to queen, an opportunity that came to her because Vashti, her predecessor, refused to appear at an earlier feast. Whatever Vashti's reasons, whether she was justified or not, the king clearly wanted to contrast the new queen with the previous one. Xerxes celebrates his own delight by sharing it with the entire kingdom, declaring a holiday and giving gifts to the populace. These feasts had a political purpose as well. They highlighted the king's power and wealth, and the gifts cemented his favor with the populace at large. This feast resulted in Esther's name becoming known throughout the kingdom. Through all this, she kept her ethnicity secret.

"Esther had kept secret her family background and nationality just as Mordecai had told her to do, for she continued to follow Mordecai's instructions as she had done when he was bringing her up" (verse 20).

"During the time Mordecai was sitting at the king's gate, Bigthana and Teresh, two of the king's officers who guarded the doorway, became angry and conspired to assassinate King Xerxes. But Mordecai found out about the plot and told Queen Esther, who in turn reported it to the king, giving credit to Mordecai. And when the report was investigated and found to be true, the two officials were impaled on poles. All this was recorded in the book of the annals in the presence of the king" (verses 20–23).

We sometimes overlook the seriousness of the plot Mordecai overheard. We may mistake doorkeepers as glorified ushers, but in fact they served a serious security function: they controlled who entered a secured area, in this case the palace. The doorkeepers themselves had access to the palace and were positioned to give entry to someone who might be a party to their plot. If you don't think so, contemplate for a moment that "doorkeepers" at the White House belong to the Secret Service. So this represented a significant threat. And any threat to Xerxes also threatens his queen. Mordecai warned Esther, who relayed word of the plot to the king himself, mentioning Mordecai as the source of her information.

Conspirators so vocal as Bigthana and Theresh were bound to have left other evidence, which the palace guard quickly discovered, and verified the existence of a plot against Xerxes. Justice was brutal and swift. Every ruler needs to know whom he can count on, so the whole incident was entered into the official royal chronicle.

We know the story of Esther so well because it is finely crafted and compelling. We encounter this episode here because the author wants to lay a foundation for the king's favor in the next phase of the story, where the villain of the piece makes his appearance.

"After these events, King Xerxes honored Haman son of Hammedatha, the Agagite, elevating him and giving him a seat of honor higher than that of all the other nobles" (Esther 3:1).

Once again we encounter a familiar setting, the (alien) power behind the throne. Not as elaborate or detailed as a story framework, it is more a character type. By this time in Bible history, we have seen it at least three times. In a positive light, we have Joseph and Daniel. Both were captives (aliens) who rose above the other advisors, giving them great influence over the kingdom. In a negative light, we have Jezebel, the Phoenician princess who becomes queen of Israel, a position of prestige but little official power. However, at crucial junctures it is clear that though Ahab may rule Israel, Jezebel rules Ahab.

In this case, Xerxes appoints Haman, who is not Persian, to the highest place of authority, next to the king himself. Will he be positive or negative? Even though he has done nothing positive or negative at this point in the narrative, the author has already signaled the danger that lies ahead by informing us that Haman is an Agagite. We do not know for certain whether this refers to the town of Agag, or whether it designates Haman as a descendant of Agag, king of the Amalekites. In either case, it almost certainly indicates that Haman is an enemy of the Jews, as the Amalekites have come to represent the archenemies of the Jewish people. There is no other reason to mention this. And as the story unfolds, certainly Haman fits the part of the archenemy of the Jews.

Rivals

"All the royal officials at the king's gate knelt down and paid honor to Haman, for the king had commanded this concerning him. But Mordecai would not kneel down or pay him honor" (Esther 3:2).

Despite repeated attempts to explain his behavior, Mordecai's refusal to bow before Haman remains a mystery. There are a number of explanations, with little or no evidence to support them. Certainly, within the story as we have it, Mordecai and Haman represent the Jews and the enemies of the Jews respectively. In fact, four times the text will refer to Haman as "the enemy of the Jews."

It's possible that the author of this story intends us to see this as a reenactment of David and Goliath, with Mordecai as the lowly David and Haman, with his power as viceroy, as a boastful and arrogant Goliath. If that is correct, then Mordecai's defiance of Haman's vanity by refusing to bow mirrors David's willingness to challenge Goliath's boasting and arrogance. Without doubt, it initiates a struggle between the two men, with Israel's safety hanging in the balance.

"Then the royal officials at the king's gate asked Mordecai, 'Why do you disobey the king's command?' Day after day they spoke to him but he refused to comply. Therefore they told Haman about it to see whether Mordecai's behavior would be tolerated, for he had told them he was a Jew" (verses 3, 4).

Wherever an absolute monarch reigns, palace intrigue surrounds the throne. Power corrupts, and the appetite for power corrodes the character and erodes friendship. Perhaps Mordecai's fellow servants found him pleasant enough personally. Perhaps they held no hostility against Jews. But when Haman took offense at Mordecai's defiance, the others saw opportunity. Haman stood second only to the king, so he could do much to aid anyone he favored. And clearly, he would favor anyone who could find a way for him to avenge himself on Mordecai. That Mordecai was Jewish simply supplied an excuse for his fellows to single him out, a convenient reason to suggest he was arrogant. From their perspective, two birds, one stone—curry favor with Haman and eliminate a potential rival. So they tell Haman, and the effect of this knowledge reveals the depth of his depravity.

"When Haman saw that Mordecai would not kneel down or pay him honor, he was enraged. Yet having learned who Mordecai's people were, he scorned the idea of killing only Mordecai. Instead Haman looked for a way to destroy all Mordecai's people, the Jews, throughout the whole kingdom of Xerxes" (verses 5, 6).

Exacting punishment for wrongdoing is one thing; wreaking vengeance on a man's family is quite another. But even that will not salve the wound to Haman's immense pride. He must destroy an entire *people!* We tend to think of genocide or ethnic cleansing as evils peculiar to our own day. In ancient times such heinous acts were commonplace. In fact, throughout the history of mankind, extermination of one's foes was something to boast about. But even in that context, Haman's ambition was shocking. After all, he was not the king. Mordecai and his people had not murdered innumerable members of Haman's kin or clan. He had offended Haman's *pride!* So Haman's reaction was diabolical.

He cannot, however, tell Xerxes that. Kings are allowed great personal pride, but the second-in-command is supposed to be concerned with the dignity of the king, not his own. If Haman wants the king to bless his extermination of the Jews, the king has to believe that Haman is protecting the royal interest, not settling his own personal scores. And Haman demonstrates the skills that propelled him to such lofty heights of power as he presents the case to Xerxes.

"Then Haman said to King Xerxes, 'There is a certain people dispersed among the peoples in all the provinces of your kingdom who keep themselves separate. Their customs are different from those of all other people, and they do not obey the king's laws; it is not in the king's best interest to tolerate them. If it pleases the king, let a decree be issued to destroy them, and I will give ten thousand talents of silver to the king's administrators for the royal treasury' " (verses 8, 9).

Haman's appeal demonstrates his skill at court politics. He portrays the Jews—though he doesn't mention them by name, "a certain people dispersed"—as dangerous rebels, disobedient to the king's decrees, and so it is "not in the king's best interest to tolerate them." Haman suggests that this dangerous group be destroyed and then offers to pay for it! He does not mention how the plunder of this operation will be divided. No doubt he planned to take pleasure in the Jews' extinction and profit by it at the same time.

Death decree

"So the king took his signet ring from his finger and gave it to Haman son of Hammedatha, the Agagite, the enemy of the Jews. 'Keep the money,' the king said to Haman, 'and do with the people as you please.' Then on the thirteenth day of the first month the royal secretaries were summoned. They wrote out in the script of each province and in the language of each people all Haman's orders to the king's satraps, the governors of the various provinces and the nobles of the various peoples. These were written in the name of King Xerxes himself and sealed with his own ring" (verses 10–12).

The king's signet ring would be pressed into hot wax on the copies of the royal decree, to authenticate it as the legal decree of the Persian Empire. Throughout the vast empire—from modern-day Libya, Egypt, and Macedonia in the west to India in the east—the king's decree would be posted and read.

"Dispatches were sent by couriers to all the king's provinces with the order to destroy, kill and annihilate all the Jews—young and old, women and children—on a single day, the thirteenth day of the twelfth month, the month of Adar, and to plunder their goods" (verse 13).

The plan was as simple as it was diabolical. On the appointed day, it would be open season on Jews. Besides the king's command for them to be killed, there was additional incentive: plunder. If their neighbors' envy wasn't enough to ensure their deaths, then their greed would surely finish the job.

"The couriers went out, spurred on by the king's command, and the edict was issued in the citadel of Susa. The king and Haman sat down to drink, but the city of Susa was bewildered" (verse 15).

The Persian Courier Service did indeed move with great haste. In order to make rapid communications possible across the vast spaces of the empire, the emperor Darius I had built a royal road that spanned the realm from east to west. Much like the famous Pony Express, more than 111 posts with fresh horses lined the road at intervals, making it possible for the couriers to ride across the entire empire in seven days. Since Susa was centrally located, we can assume that Xerxes' decree reached the farthest outposts of the empire in four to five days at the most.

Given the tremendous distances traveled with such speed, the courier service was famous in its day. The Greek historian, Herodotus, wrote of them, "Neither snow nor rain nor heat nor gloom of night stays these couriers from the swift completion of their appointed rounds."

If it sounds familiar, that's because the saying is inscribed on the James Farley Post Office in New York City and is considered the unofficial motto of the U.S. Postal Service.

Note the contrast between the leaders, Haman and the king, and the rest of the capital city after this lethal decree goes out. Haman and the king apparently celebrate this achievement with a drink, while the rest of the capital ponders the consequences of an open hunting season on one of the many people groups that make up the empire. This was not business as usual for the Persian Empire. As mentioned earlier, Persians allowed freedom of religion, unlike the empires before them, and many after. With this decree, that policy seemed threatened. If you were not Persian, the unspoken question had to be, who would be next? As the capital of the empire, Susa would be home to representatives of virtually every conquered nation. The "city of Susa was bewildered," indeed. The couriers did their work, and soon, Jews throughout Persia were in a state of shock.

"When Mordecai learned of all that had been done, he tore his clothes, put on sackcloth and ashes, and went out into the city, wailing loudly and bitterly. But he went only as far as the king's gate, because no one clothed in sackcloth was allowed to enter it. In every province to which the edict and order of the king came, there was great mourning among the Jews, with fasting, weeping and wailing. Many lay in sackcloth and ashes. When Esther's eunuchs and female attendants came and told her about Mordecai, she was in great distress" (Esther 4:1–4).

As Esther later makes clear, ordinary people, even in royal employ, did not have ready access to those in the palace. Since Mordecai could not simply send her a message or visit her, she apparently had those in her service go and watch carefully to see how he fared. The news of his distress came to her rapidly through her servants. She sent clean clothing to him, but he refused to wear it. Sensing that something more serious afflicted Mordecai, she sent Hathach, a eunuch who was assigned to attend her, to speak with Mordecai.

"Mordecai told him everything that had happened to him, including the exact amount of money Haman had promised to pay into the royal treasury for the destruction of the Jews. He also gave him a copy of the text of the edict for their annihilation, which had been published in Susa, to show to Esther and explain it to her, and he told him to instruct her to go into the king's presence to beg for mercy and plead with him for her people" (verses 7, 8).

Jews across the entire empire mourned, and yet Esther knew nothing about it. How could this be?

The cordial drink shared by Haman and Xerxes, in contrast with the perplexity in the surrounding city, demonstrates the isolation of the palace as a world of its own, a place quite apart from the concerns of the ordinary Persian subject. Whatever mayhem may have been taking place in the streets, only conquest by an enemy would trouble those in the royal residence.

And besides, Esther had not "made known her people," at Mordecai's instructions. Apparently, even her closest attendants within the palace did not know her secret, else they would have known to inform her of Haman's plot. When Hathach returned, not only with his report from Mordecai but with a written copy of the deadly decree, it must have been a terrific shock. And the suggestion that she go to Xerxes, unbidden, supplied a second emotional shock. It was all too much.

She sent Hathach back, explaining that should she go to Xerxes, as Mordecai suggested, she might well die. If Xerxes did not accept her, she would be killed on the spot. This was not arbitrary or barbaric; it was security. Just imagine what would happen to someone who suddenly appeared in the Oval Office of the White House while the president was busy at his desk! If that person appeared to be a threat, he or she might well end up dead.

That was only the first obstacle she faced. If the king extended his scepter to her in welcome, she would then have to somehow persuade him to rescind his decree—something that, by Persian law, he could not do. What could she do? Since he had already acceded to the extermination of her people, the king might well add her to the toll. She concluded her message to Mordecai by saying, "Thirty days have passed since I was called to go to the king" (verse 11).

During that thirty days, the death decree had been signed, sealed, and dispatched throughout the kingdom. She did not know if perhaps the king had become displeased with her; perhaps he had discovered her Jewish heritage. Perhaps Haman had turned the king against her. The palace was its own small kingdom, with scores of dignitaries and servants, multiple little self-contained dominions with their own internal politics and intrigues. We have already seen that the affairs of state did not always penetrate into the queen's domain.

But Mordecai warns her that this death decree will not pass over her door.

"Do not think that because you are in the king's house you alone of all the Jews will escape. For if you remain silent at this time, relief and deliverance for the Jews will arise from another place, but you and your father's family will perish. And who knows but that you have come to your royal position for such a time as this?" (verses 13, 14).

If Esther had any thoughts of surviving by remaining silent, Mordecai dispels them. He knows the depth of Haman's anger and depravity, something she likely would not have seen, given her station. Mordecai knows that Haman will not rest until the last Jew has been eliminated, so he warns her that she will not survive. But he does not limit his appeal to her basest instincts.

Neither does he tell her that she is indispensable because of her rank. Instead, he appeals to her highest aspirations.

We have already noted that many believed that the really devout, "good" Jews had already departed for Judea and Jerusalem. And Mordecai had counseled Esther to conceal her Jewish connection. Up to this point, we have seen no indication that Mordecai and Esther were what we would call "observant" Jews. Yet here we have an unconditional expression of faith in God. "Deliverance will come," Mordecai tells her. Not that it *might* come or it *could* come. No, it "*will come.*" Mordecai thus presents the situation not as a last resort but as an *opportunity* afforded Esther because of her exalted rank as queen, as a *high calling*.

We have already seen Esther's beauty of character as well as of appearance, so her positive response to his appeal is totally in character. She will not use her protected status as an excuse to stand aloof, or even to repudiate her people, but will risk all on their behalf.

"Go, gather together all the Jews who are in Susa, and fast for me. Do not eat or drink for three days, night or day. I and my attendants will fast as you do. When this is done, I will go to the king, even though it is against the law. And if I perish, I perish" (verse 16).

These are not the words of a shy orphan girl, or even of a beautiful princess; this is the declaration of a heroine! It cannot have escaped her that Vashti had lost her position as queen and been banished from the palace for *not* appearing before Xerxes when summoned. And now she planned to seek his attention *without* being summoned.

Dinner for three

Having committed herself, she now must come up with a plan to outmaneuver Haman, whose political skills have put him at the pinnacle of power, having prevailed over other cunning politicians. The task she accepted would require wisdom as well as courage.

"On the third day Esther put on her royal robes and stood in the inner court of the palace. . . . When [the king] saw Queen Esther standing in the court, he was pleased with her and held out to her the gold scepter" (Esther 5:1, 2).

You may have noticed that the phrase "she found favor," or "he was pleased with her," occurs repeatedly throughout this narrative. And we have seen that it arises more from her character and demeanor than her physical appearance. The king still has a harem—she is not the only attractive woman available to him. Indeed, her statement that she has not been summoned to the royal presence in thirty days implies that the king has been occupied with others of his wives or concubines. But Esther's sweet spirit makes her welcome at any time. From her perspective, she has survived the first hurdle.

"So Esther approached and touched the tip of the scepter. Then the king asked, 'What is it, Queen Esther? What is your request? Even up to half the kingdom, it will be given you' " (verses 2, 3).

Centuries later, Herod will make the same offer to Salome. Offering up to half the kingdom was understood as hyperbole, even at the time. Neither Xerxes nor Herod had any intention of surrendering half their kingdom. It was simply an expression of how well the petitioner has pleased the king. Even with this extravagant offer, Xerxes could not have anticipated that Esther wanted something that would affect his entire empire and pit her against his chief adviser, Haman. An ancient observer, had he known what Esther sought to accomplish, and recognizing the depth both of Haman's hatred and his influence, would have been awed by the enormity of the task the young queen had accepted. How could she hope to prevail? What possible strategy could she employ?

" 'If it pleases the king,' replied Esther, 'let the king, together with Haman, come today to a banquet I have prepared for him' " (verse 4).

Why did she invite Haman? At first blush, one would think she would want to get the king alone, to charm and persuade him without Haman being any the wiser. But Esther knows what she is doing. This is not simply an assignation of the king with a member of his harem. Esther has something more on her mind. Her task involves the empire at large, and, Haman, as the king's most trusted adviser, will have his say. If he were excluded, he might become suspicious, might decide to investigate the queen's possible motivations and discover her Jewish roots.

But if he is included in a banquet with the royal couple, he will be flattered. The honor alone will likely soothe his swollen ego, and, being present, he will have no reason for suspicion.

Perhaps Esther wanted to expose Haman's base motives, wanted the king to see that Haman was motivated by his personal pride rather than any concern for Xerxes. If Xerxes saw that, Haman would lose his influence, and perhaps much more. Kings are all too accustomed to those who seek royal favor in order to use imperial power for their own ends.

And there may be one more reason. Part of a king's duties includes the command of armies and sending men to their death. For the Persian emperor, even when present at battle, this was largely an abstraction. Positioned a great distance behind the skirmish lines, surrounded by his personal guard, he could see the ant-like figures fighting in the distance; but for the most part he avoided the sounds, the emotions, and the stench of battle.

Haman framed the issuing of the death decree in the terms of an abstraction. Those to be eliminated were "*a certain people dispersed,*" Haman had said. "*They do not obey the king's laws.*" Basically, it was a police action—getting rid of what some would call "undesirable elements" centuries later.

If Esther could get Xerxes to see this in personal terms, to see up close Haman's hatred for her, a flesh-and-blood woman, as well as for all her people, the king might be repulsed by it. A banquet for three, in her quarters, would be very personal indeed.

"As they were drinking wine, the king again asked Esther, 'Now what is your petition? It will be given you. And what is your request? Even up to half the kingdom, it will be granted.' Esther replied, 'My petition and my request is this: If the king regards me with favor and if it pleases the king to grant my petition and fulfill my request, let the king and Haman come tomorrow to the banquet I will prepare for them. Then I will answer the king's question' " (verses 6–8).

Evidently the king found the first banquet quite pleasing. He repeats his offer to grant whatever Esther wants in the most extravagant terms. So why does she not make her request, but instead invites Haman and the king to yet another banquet, to be held the next night?

Again and again we have seen that men are mystified when it comes to women. Perhaps Esther realizes that mystery is one of a woman's greatest assets when it comes to dealing with men. Perhaps she believes that a second pleasant evening will make the king even more ready to grant her request. Perhaps she used this first evening to take the measure of both Haman and the relationship between the two men. Perhaps she wants more time to pray, to contemplate, and to formulate her strategy. As we almost always find with the portrayal of women in the Bible, we simply do not know.

Whatever her reasoning, the events of the next twenty-four hours could hardly have gone better for Esther and her plans. But none of these were things she could have planned. Considering everything that took place, it seems obvious that God must have intervened.

"Haman went out that day happy and in high spirits. But when he saw Mordecai at the king's gate and observed that he neither rose nor showed fear in his presence, he was filled with rage against Mordecai" (verse 9).

If there is any doubt concerning Haman's bloated sense of pride, this verse eliminates it. Having just come from a private banquet, with only the king and queen in attendance besides himself, Haman should have been on top of the world. Surely, being ignored by someone as lowly as Mordecai is something he should have written off as unimportant. But Haman's immense pride cannot stand even the slightest irritation. Mordecai ignores him, and Haman is inconsolable.

Haman goes home and recounts all of the privileges of riches that the king has given him, and then he mentions this private banquet with the king and queen. "But all this gives me no satisfaction as long as I see that Jew Mordecai sitting at the king's gate" (verse 13).

Really? Riches, power, authority, and privilege, with singular recognition—and one man refusing to bow negates all of that? Such is the poisonous effect of pride. In a scene reminiscent of Ahab and Jezebel, Haman pours his discontent in front of his wife, and she suggests a particularly nasty type of revenge: that he should erect a scaffold fifty cubits—seventy-five feet—high, to make his enemy's corpse visible all over Susa.

Then his wife suggests that he should speak to the king in the morning about having Mordecai hung on his gallows.

But here God clearly intervenes. The inclusion of the book of Esther into the Jewish canon was controversial because God is not specifically mentioned in the entire book. There's the three days of fasting and prayer but no explicit mention of God. And yet, only God could have arranged these amazing events that took place within such a tight time window in order to achieve these dramatic results.

For some reason, the king cannot sleep that night. An old proverb says, "Uneasy lies the head that bears the crown." One reason for that royal unease is that people continually want to take power from you.

"That night the king could not sleep; so he ordered the book of the chronicles, the record of his reign, to be brought in and read to him. It was found recorded there that Mordecai had exposed Bigthana and Teresh, two of the king's officers who guarded the doorway, who had conspired to assassinate King Xerxes. 'What honor and recognition has Mordecai received for this?' the king asked. 'Nothing has been done for him,' his attendants answered" (Esther 6:1–3).

So the king awakes the next morning acutely aware that Mordecai has saved his life and has received no reward for that singular service. As soon as he arrives at the palace, the king looks around to find someone to suggest how he should reward Mordecai for saving the king's life. At that point, Haman walks in, primed to request that Mordecai be hanged from the highest gallows. It is difficult to imagine a more dramatic contrast between the two men's intentions. Before Haman can speak, the king asks him, "What shall be done to the man whom the king delights to honor?" (verse 6).

Haman can only think of one person worthy of receiving the royal reward—himself. And so he prescribes as a reward precisely what he himself desires.

"Have them bring a royal robe the king has worn and a horse the king has ridden, one with a royal crest placed on its head. Then let the robe and horse be entrusted to one of the king's most noble princes. Let them robe the man the king delights to honor, and lead him on the horse through the city streets, proclaiming before him, 'This is what is done for the man the king delights to honor!' " (verses 8, 9).

As a child, I was often told that the best gift to give to a friend is one that I would desire for myself. In that spirit, Haman designed the perfect gift for Mordecai. But this, of course, is where the irony sets in. As "one of the king's most noble princes," Haman is delegated to lead Mordecai mounted on the royal steed and clothed in royal raiment; and he, Haman, will have to call everyone's attention to the unparalleled honor being paid to his mortal enemy.

For a man as proud as Haman, this may have been more painful than being hanged from the gallows. He must now pay homage to the one man who continually refused to bow to him. Of all the plots used in telling stories, the one many enjoy the most is the one called "the biter bitten." Sometimes we refer to it as poetic justice. And here it is, in spades. How Haman's pride must have suffered, how much it must have burned him to be forced to lead his mortal enemy through the street and declare him to be the recipient of the king's greatest delight and favor.

We do not know, as mentioned earlier, what Esther's purpose was in delaying her request until the second banquet. But we know for certain that God used it to the greatest possible advantage. Not only does He bring Mordecai's loyal service to the attention of the king, but He also humiliates the prideful Haman. And no doubt this deeply humiliating experience primed Haman for what will happen at the second banquet.

"His advisers and his wife Zeresh said to him, 'Since Mordecai, before whom your downfall has started, is of Jewish origin, you cannot stand against him—you will surely come to ruin!' " (verse 13).

As Haman had opined his humiliation the night before, he now shared this new slight with his wife and his friends. They say his "downfall has started" before Mordecai, foreshadowing his doom. And then they proclaim a fearful prophecy: that if Mordecai was a Jew, Haman would not prevail. We do not know for sure, but perhaps there lingered in their memory the story of Daniel and the lions' den. Surely it was a cautionary tale for those who would oppose the Jews.

"While they were still talking with him, the king's eunuchs arrived and hurried Haman away to the banquet Esther had prepared" (verse 14).

"While they were still talking with him . . ." The biblical author thus drives the narrative forward, giving Haman no opportunity to fully comprehend what he's been told, to process the information, or even to prepare himself mentally, before the king's messages sweep him forward to the next banquet, where he will meet his doom.

Imagine Haman's emotional turmoil as he attended another exclusive banquet with the queen and king. Within twenty-four hours he has experienced exultation at the first banquet, frustration that Mordecai still does not bow, anticipation as he orders a gallows for his hated foe, exhilaration as he prescribes the reward he expects to receive, humiliation as he leads Mordecai through the streets, declaring the king's recognition of the man he most despises, and now again exultation as the guest of the king and queen. And he has yet to receive the greatest shock.

An adversary and an enemy

At first, the banquet must have helped settle Haman's raw nerves. Excellent food, pleasant conversation, the attention of his king, and the company of a beautiful woman. After the meal, Xerxes repeated his offer to grant Esther any request, "Up to half of my kingdom." If he thought about it at all, Haman probably expected her to request a title or position for a relative, or expanded quarters for herself, perhaps silver or gold, or more servants. Most likely, he was considering his own desires. So he probably awaited Esther's response with mild curiosity. That would change.

"If I have found favor with you, Your Majesty, and if it pleases you, grant me my life—this is my petition. And spare my people—this is my request. For I and my people have been sold to be destroyed, killed and annihilated. If we had merely been sold as male and female slaves, I would have kept quiet, because no such distress would justify disturbing the king" (Esther 7:3, 4).

One cannot help but wonder what went through the mind of each of the two men listening to her request. We have some idea of the king's thoughts, because he gives voice to them.

"Who is he? Where is he—the man who has dared to do such a thing?" (verse 5).

Clearly, the king is surprised and shocked by the queen's request, even though he had signed the decree. He finds it astonishing that someone would presume to kill his queen and her people. And once again, the beauty of her character stands out. "If we had been sold for male and female slaves, I would've held my peace" (verse 4, WEB). Even in this extreme peril, she retains her humility.

She is willing that she and her people serve the king. This directly contradicts Haman's claim that the Jews refused to follow the king's laws and that they were therefore essentially in rebellion. Xerxes is indignant and furious. He wants to know the identity of the perpetrator.

Now imagine Haman's thoughts. He probably believes this beautiful creature is shallow and frivolous. But with each word she speaks, he becomes more and more alarmed. And the king's reaction must have sent Haman into the depths of despair. At this point Esther delivers the fatal blow.

"An adversary and an enemy! This vile Haman!" (verse 6; emphasis added).

Upon hearing this, and seeing the confirmation of guilt written on Haman's face, Xerxes faces a new and frightening reality. Haman, whom he had trusted implicitly—even giving him the royal signet and allowing him to write the decree that condemned the Jews—is completely untrustworthy. Haman has repaid the king's trust by using his authority for himself, and not in the king's interest. Perhaps as a means of marshaling his thoughts and controlling his great rage, the king walks out into the garden.

The king realizes that, in contrast to the scheming Haman, his beautiful wife, Esther, had proclaimed that she would not use her position to protect herself from serving the king. She had declared that if she and her people had been sold as slaves, she would not have objected. This is so extraordinary that it brings to mind Paul's hymn to Christ in Philippians 2, where he reveals that Christ did not consider His station as God something to be held onto, but rather was willing to become a servant. Of course, Christ's sacrifice was infinitely greater than what Esther proposed for herself, yet it does remain a striking parallel.

Haman recognized the king's fury, and, like many bullies, when confronted with his own death, he demonstrated his craven nature, flinging himself literally and figuratively upon the mercy of the queen.

At this moment the king returns from the garden, where he was no doubt pacing about pondering the consequences of what had just transpired. And here he finds Haman apparently in physical contact with the queen. Whatever shreds of regard for Haman remained in the king's mind, finding Haman in such a position swept away all notions of mercy.

"The king exclaimed, 'Will he even molest the queen while she is with me in the house?' As soon as the word left the king's mouth, they covered Haman's face" (verse 8).

"They covered Haman's face." It is an age-old custom to cover the head of one who is about to be executed, and that is what the guards are doing. For anyone to assault a member of the royal family was a capital crime, and in ancient times the king was judge and jury in any case. So the king's declaration about Haman assaulting the queen served as a death sentence. Only the means of execution remained to be specified. The eunuch who was apparently part of the king's Secret Service detail had a suggestion.

"Then Harbona, one of the eunuchs attending the king, said, 'A pole reaching to a height of fifty cubits stands by Haman's house. He had it set up for Mordecai, who spoke up to help the king' " (verse 9).

It is interesting that the royal servants were more aware of Haman's machinations than either the king or the queen. They also seemed to know who could be trusted and whose ambitions were treacherous. There appears to have been no love lost among the royal servants for Haman, not only because they immediately covered his head in preparation for execution, but because they made known to the king the most fitting penalty. Harbona knows about Haman's gallows and its intended victim, but the king does not. The eunuch mentions the gallows and also points out that Mordecai, "who spoke up to help the king," had been Haman's target. The king, even more furious, wastes neither time nor words: "Impale him on it!" (verse 9).

Haman's death precipitates a complete reversal within the kingdom. The king awards Haman's house to Queen Esther. He then elevates Mordecai to the position Haman had held, that of chief advisor to the king, which included giving him the signet ring retrieved from Haman.

But a few things remain to be done. Esther once again seeks the king's attention unbidden. "Esther again pleaded with the king, falling at his feet and weeping. She begged him to put an end to the evil plan of Haman the Agagite, which he had devised against the Jews. Then the king extended the gold scepter" (Esther 8:3, 4).

The timid Esther has become ever more bold. The first time she came in, she waited silently until the king extended his scepter to her. This time, perhaps spurred on by the peril of her people, and reassured by the king's generous treatment of her and Mordecai, she petitions him for redress of the evil Haman had devised, even before the king extends his scepter.

He responds in signal fashion. Before, he had let Haman write the decree condemning the Jews; Xerxes now gives Mordecai permission to write a decree in his name that allows the Jews to defend themselves. And just as before, the scribes are summoned and the decree is inscribed. Couriers are dispatched to distribute the decree throughout the vast empire.

From Egypt to the Hindus River, the Jews rejoice. They will be allowed to protect themselves and even to take plunder from those they defeat. The incentives now have been reversed. Those who might have sought to gain by destroying the Jews now not only face a potentially armed enemy but risk forfeiting all of their own possessions should they fail. The decrees of the Persian king cannot be reversed, so the date for the extermination of Jews remained. But the new decree finesses this law by countering the first decree with another. Both remain in force; neither is reversed. Yet the effect is to negate the first decree.

Even in the capital of Susa, some still sought the destruction of the Jews, and among those were, not surprisingly, Haman's ten sons. They were listed among the some five hundred men who were killed by the Jews within the capital. Apparently, Susa was the site of considerable opposition to Mordecai and the Jews, because Esther requested that the Jews in the capital be given a second day to fight back against their enemies. The text tells us that on that day, an additional three hundred enemies of the Jews were killed. But the author is careful to point out that "they didn't lay hand on the plunder." As Abraham did when he rescued Lot, the Jews wanted to make it clear that this was self-defense, not seeking material gain.

No one could blame them if they had taken plunder. After all, they had been living peaceably with their neighbors, and they had not sought this opportunity for conflict. On the contrary, it was Haman who sought their demise. Probably the extra resistance within the capital indicates the breadth and depth of the political struggle for power. No doubt Haman had allies who were loath to relinquish their influence with the king.

At this point it would seem that everything that has been wrong has been turned right again. Haman and his sons are dead; Mordecai has been elevated to the highest place in the kingdom next to the king; and the Jews have been preserved. But Esther had requested one more thing: "Let Haman's ten sons be impaled on poles."

To the modern ear, this sounds like a shocking request coming from the demure queen. Has this virtuous woman suddenly become vengeful and bloodthirsty? Remember, Haman did not want simply to kill Mordecai and his relatives; he wanted to wipe out all the Jewish people in the Persian Empire. This would effectively have eliminated Judaism from the world.

Esther wanted to make sure that no one would be tempted into such a heinous act again. Haman's sons were already dead. She wanted them hanged from the gallows as a warning to enemies of the Jews. Hanging the dead bodies rather than giving them burial amounted to extinguishing Haman's name and posterity forever. There would be no monuments, no memorials over their remains. No place for sympathizers to go and mourn. "This," the decaying bodies would proclaim, "is what happens to those who conspire against the Jews."

For many days, all the citizens of Susa would be reminded of Haman's perfidy and of his shameful end by the sight of the bodies of his ten sons slowly consumed by vultures and eventually becoming only a pile of bones.

We noted that had Haman succeeded, this would have resulted in the extermination of the Jews. Their extinction would include the Old Testament. The thirty-nine books we call the Old Testament are the oldest documents in continuous use in the world. They survived because the Jewish people survived. And the Jewish people survived because Esther, at great personal risk, took the initiative.

In several ways Esther looks very much like the strong partner of Joseph. Both were exiles, far from home, who rose to positions of influence and ultimately saved Israel. They both had come into the kingdom for just such a time.

We tell the story of Esther as the tale of a beautiful girl who wins the heart of the king and uses her feminine wiles to influence him. But what we see on closer examination is a woman of amazing humility, whose winsome character and shrewd reason persuade a king and rescue God's chosen people.

This story also serves to caution us about our faith in our own judgments of who is devout and who is not. And it gives comfort to those who feel themselves "left behind." Mordecai's caution to Esther warns us as well: "Who knows if you haven't come to the kingdom for such a time as this?" God places each one of us where, if we devote our lives and talents to Him, we will play an indispensable role in His great plan of salvation.

TWELVE

MARY OF NAZARETH
A Change of Schedule

We teach children to pray over the small things in their lives—lost pets, and even lost toys. As adults, we often reserve prayer for the supposedly more important things in our lives, like the significant decisions we need to make. We tend to think that God is not really interested in our smaller concerns. Is this true? That question was settled nearly two thousand years ago in a small town in Galilee. If not for the Gospel of John, we would never have known about this celebration, or have seen the significance God places on even the small things in our lives.

It is a simple story that almost everyone knows. The wedding was held in Cana, a village not far from Jesus' home in Nazareth. John tells us that Jesus' mother was there, and he adds that Jesus and His disciples were also present. Jewish weddings in the first century were weeklong affairs, where friends, neighbors, and relatives feasted and danced and generally celebrated the new union. Exactly how far into the celebration this event took place we are not told. The account, like much of John, is simple and straightforward—deceptively so.

> When the wine was gone, Jesus' mother said to Him, "They have no more wine."
>
> "Woman, why do you involve me?" Jesus replied. "My hour has not yet come" (John 2:3, 4).

The marvelous economy of John conceals within these few words an amazing amount of content. First of all, it simply says, "When the wine was gone," as if that was an expected occurrence. But it was not. When the wine ran out, the celebration was over, and if it ran out before the appointed time, it would be a great embarrassment to the host and to the newlywed couple. John tells us none of that, because he expects his audience to already know it. In our time, it would be something like the wedding cake not showing up for the reception. Everyone expected it, and its absence would be an occasion of note.

Next, we have the simple statement that when the wine ran out, "Jesus' mother said to Him, 'They have no more wine' " (verse 3). The third-person pronoun "they" tells us that whether they were related to the bride and groom or not, Jesus and His mother were not officially part of the wedding party—rather, they were guests. If there is embarrassment over the lack of wine, it cannot be considered their responsibility. Jesus' reply indicates that. "Why do you involve Me?" He asks. In our language, that would sound something like, "Why do you mention that? It is not my problem."

But then Jesus says six significant words: *"My hour has not yet come"* (verse 4; emphasis added).

If we were not familiar with the Gospel of John, these words would simply seem odd or out of place. What does "His hour" have to do with the wedding's lack of wine? And again, unless we expect something unusual from Jesus, what is the purpose of this whole exchange?

As indicated earlier, this story occurs only in the Gospel of John. In this Gospel, the concept of Jesus' "time" or "hour" occurs repeatedly. It appears to refer to a divine schedule for Jesus' life and ministry. In John 7, Jesus' brothers taunt Him and urge Him to go to Jerusalem so that His disciples may see His "mighty works." We are explicitly told that they do not believe in Him, and apparently they think He has delusions of grandeur, which they want to dispel. But Jesus refuses, telling them it is not time—not His hour—for Him to go.

Several days later, when He does go to the Feast of Tabernacles, His preaching enrages the crowd. But we are told, "They sought therefore to take Him; but no one laid a hand on Him, because His hour had not yet come" (John 7:30, WEB).

When the time is right, when His hour does arrive, He takes action and will not be deterred. In chapter 12 of the Gospel of John, after we have been informed that the Jews are actively seeking to kill Jesus, He tells Andrew and Philip, "The time has come for the Son of Man to be glorified" (John 12:23, WEB). Jesus makes it clear that this glorification means His death when He says, "Now my soul is troubled. What shall I say? 'Father, save me from this time?' But for this cause I came to this time" (verse 27, WEB).

More than a dozen times in the Gospel of John, Jesus refers to His hour or His time, and He refuses to deviate from it, even when following this timeline means meeting His death. So when He tells His mother, "My hour is not yet," He is speaking of this divine schedule. That's what makes the episode, even beyond the miracle that is to follow, so significant.

He says His hour has not yet come, but He acts *anyway*. It is the only time in John's Gospel that He deviates from the divinely appointed schedule.

Exactly what Mary expected, we do not know. But she knows her Son will act. Mary's next words demonstrate her confidence that Jesus will honor her request.

"His mother said to the servants, 'Do whatever He tells you' " (John 2:5).

Of course, we know the story. Jesus tells the servants to fill several large jars with water. Then He tells them to take some of this "water" to the master of the feast. The master then tastes the wine—for that is what it has become—and declares it to be better than the wine served earlier.

If the focus of this book and this chapter were on Jesus and His miracles, we would have a great deal more to say about the details of this amazing story. For instance, we would point out that the specific vessels to be filled with water were those used for ceremonial cleansing. And we would note that wine in the New Testament is often associated with blood, specifically with Jesus' blood.

In addition, we would point out that one of the great themes of the Gospel of John is the substitution of Jesus and His sacrifice for the Old Testament rituals. So here, the "wine" that Jesus provides in these vessels for cleansing, and which is better than the other wine already served at the feast, is an intentional metaphor for the blood of Jesus. His blood is a better remedy than the Old Testament rituals. There are many other things we would point out, if the miracle itself, rather than Mary's actions which occasioned it, were the focus.

But here we're talking about Mary seizing the initiative. Mary is a remarkable character throughout the Gospels, but we primarily see her in an accepting and somewhat passive role. This is the only occasion when she is shown to take the initiative. And the results are incomparable.

You may think I'm making too much of all this. After all, Jesus may not have altered His schedule; maybe this was "just another miracle," one of the many He performed. Perhaps, if this story occurred in any of the other Gospels, that would be a telling argument. But it occurs only in John. And John, as you probably know, is different from the other three Gospels. We call the other three "synoptic," which means "to see the same," because they present the events in the life of Jesus in a very similar way. But John differs significantly in terms of both the selection and sequence of the events in Jesus' life.

One significant difference is that John does not speak of miracles. In John, these remarkable divine actions are referred to as "signs," of which only seven are recorded. As we have said before, Bible students familiar with the ancients' mindset recognize that the number seven represents completion or perfection. So these seven signs in John do not purport to be *all* of the miracles Jesus performed—John tells us in two places that He has not included all of those wonderful acts in his Gospel (see John 20:30; 21:25)—but rather, these seven signs *represent* the totality of Jesus' mission. John offers these seven signs as milestones in Jesus' complete and perfect ministry here on earth.

That is why we know this miracle at a small wedding in an obscure village packs such significance. Lest we miss its import, John concludes the episode with the following: "What Jesus did here in Cana of Galilee was the first of the signs through which He revealed His glory; and His disciples believed in Him" (John 2:11).

No matter how many times I contemplate this episode, I find it impossible to comprehend the magnitude of what has happened here. Throughout the Gospel of John, Jesus strictly adheres to this divine schedule, which He refuses to alter for any purpose. The taunts of His brothers do not move Him; crowds seeking to destroy Him cannot lay hands on Him because it is the wrong time in the schedule; and when His death is imminent, He insists on sticking to the schedule. His hour, the hour for which He has come to this earth, the hour when the most significant single event in the history of mankind must take place, this hour He will not alter. He does alter it only once—for His mother—in order to save an unknown couple and their family from embarrassment at their wedding.

Am I saying that God the Father did not foresee this request by Jesus' mother? Did God not foresee that she would request Jesus to act before His "hour"? I do not know. Jesus apparently believes that this is not a part of His schedule; His *hour has not yet come*—He says so! And yet He acts. This action is not a footnote, sidelight, or an addition. It is the first of His signs. There are only seven that signify His complete and perfect ministry on earth, and this one, this rescue of a wedding feast to save a couple from embarrassment, is incorporated into those few signs!

It seems to me that God honored Jesus' mother's request by altering the divine schedule and making the honoring of that request integral to His ministry.

Is there anything comparable throughout Scripture? If there is, it escapes me. God made the sun stand still for Joshua; He made the sun back up for Hezekiah. But these only involved material objects. These things seem remarkable to us, but for God who can call them into existence or snuff them out with a word, these are small things indeed. But to alter His divine plan, to honor the request of a woman—this boggles the imagination! In short, our prayers and choices affect eternity.

This episode reveals two amazing things about God. First, He cares even about the small things in our lives—in this case, the momentary embarrassment and discomfiture of a newlywed peasant family. And second, sometimes He will alter His eternal plans in order to grant the request of a single individual. Astonishing!

THIRTEEN

THE WOMAN AT THE WELL
DIFFERENT AS NIGHT AND DAY

She was stunned! Ordinarily, the village women drew water at dawn and dusk. So she went to the well about noon, expecting to be there alone, to avoid the upturned noses and cruel words from the other women. And then she met this man, this *Jew*—who asked her to give Him a drink! It was scandalous, and she didn't need any more scandal in her life.

Of course, you know the story. So do I. It has been told many, many times, and thousands of sermons have been preached about it. And despite all this, I read it for years without seeing its full scope and its surprising implications. You know the saying about not being able to see the forest for the trees? That's what happened to me with this episode. I knew the details (the trees) so well that I missed the bigger picture (the forest). See if you can spot it: "Now he [Jesus] had to go through Samaria. So he came to a town in Samaria called Sychar, near the plot of ground Jacob had given to His son Joseph. Jacob's well was there, and Jesus, tired as he was from the journey, sat down by the well. It was about noon. When a Samaritan woman came to draw water, Jesus said to her, 'Will you give me a drink?' " (John 4:4–7).

If you just saw it for the first time, you're saying, "Wow!" If you didn't, don't feel bad. Most people miss it, because we are looking for something else. Let me give you some clues. (1) Jesus was born in Bethlehem in Judea, so when He stops in Samaria, He is traveling in a foreign land. (2) In that foreign land, He goes to a well. (3) While at the well, He meets a member of the opposite sex. (4) He asks this person for a drink, which would require her to draw water from the well. In this case, they have a lengthy conversation, after which (5) the woman rushes home with the news about this stranger.

Yes. It's a Betrothal Narrative.

At this point you may be objecting, "But Jesus isn't a prospective bridegroom, and certainly not for *this* woman!" Hold that thought; we'll come back to it. If you find this Betrothal Narrative surprising, imagine the shock that a first-century Jew steeped in the Old Testament would feel. The scenario presented here is simply outrageous. Are *they* going to be *betrothed! Impossible!* A Jewish man cannot marry a Samaritan woman! Talking with *any* Samaritan would be scandalous, but this is a Samaritan *woman!* Don't forget, Jewish women were not allowed in the men's courtyard at the Temple. They had their own courtyard. A Samaritan woman would be considered of even lower status.

This Samaritan woman understands very well the attitudes in her day and reacts with disbelief. "The Samaritan woman said to him, 'You are a Jew and I am a Samaritan woman. How can you ask me for a drink?' (For Jews do not associate with Samaritans)" (verse 9). This editorial comment, "For Jews do not associate with Samaritans," tells us something about the audience the Gospel of John was written for. Many of them were not Jews. If they had been, this comment would not have been necessary.

As her words indicate, the woman at the well felt quite defensive. By speaking first and expressing a need, Jesus puts Himself in a vulnerable position—she could ignore Him or refuse His request. Jesus' putting her in control of the encounter increases her sense of safety. This Jewish man, rather than being haughty and superior, has requested her help. That emboldens her to ask Him how He can dare to be vulnerable with *her*.

Now that Jesus has her full attention, He tells her about the water He has to offer. "Jesus answered her, 'If you knew the gift of God and who it is that asks you for a drink, you would have asked him and he would have given you living water'" (verse 10).

A moment earlier, He had asked her for water. Now He claims to have water for *her*. He has piqued her interest.

"'Sir,' the woman said, 'you have nothing to draw with and the well is deep. Where can you get this living water?'" (verse 11).

This woman, this Samaritan, sees that He cannot be talking about water from this well—yet He offers her water. Not the unmoving water pooled in the bottom of the well, but living water. Living water was an expression Jews used to describe fresh, pure, flowing water, such as water in a stream or bubbling from a spring. Humans can dig wells, but living water comes from God in the form of rain, snow, or the flow from a spring. Only living water could be used for ritual cleansing. This well offers nothing so marvelous, even though it is associated with the legendary Jacob himself. This leads her to a shocking conclusion.

"Are you greater than our father Jacob, who gave us the well and drank from it himself, as did also his sons and his livestock?" (verse 12).

This is a rhetorical question, a question that implies an answer—that Jesus' offer exceeds the accomplishment of Jacob. Or perhaps, if water from Jacob's well gives life, then water from this strange Jewish man who talks to Samaritan women gives eternal life! And He offers it to her!

"Jesus answered, 'Everyone who drinks this water will be thirsty again, but whoever drinks the water I give them will never thirst. Indeed, the water I give them will become in them a spring of water welling up to eternal life.' The woman said to him, 'Sir, give me this water so that I won't get thirsty and have to keep coming here to draw water' " (verse 13–15).

As so many of us do, she misunderstands at first what Jesus is offering, taking it too literally, seeing it only in terms of her daily chores. If she receives this water and never thirsts, it will eliminate her daily trips to Jacob's well.

In the previous chapter of the Gospel of John, Jesus told Nicodemus He needed to be born again, born from above, and Nicodemus wanted to argue about the possibility. He could have said, "I want to be born again. Help me." But he did not. In contrast, the Samaritan woman does not argue whether or not Jesus has the water He claims. She simply requests it. Jesus longs to reveal Himself to her.

Nicodemus had said, "We know you are teacher who has come from God" (John 3:2). The Samaritan woman is on the verge of discovering that Jesus is much more. Only a few shreds of doubt remain in her mind, and Jesus is about to remove those.

"He told her, 'Go, call your husband and come back.'

" 'I have no husband,' she replied" (John 4:16, 17).

The simple fact that she comes to draw water alone in the heat of the day would lead one to surmise that the other women did not like her for some reason. She has endured condemnation and ridicule before. It would be a pity if her encounter with this apparently kind stranger ended on a sour note. But she is used to men disappointing her. So she answers Him truthfully, but carefully. That's what makes His reply so astonishing.

"Jesus said to her, 'You are right when you say you have no husband. The fact is, you have had five husbands, and the man you now have is not your husband. What you have just said is quite true' " (verses 17, 18).

This detail alone gives the story relevance to our day. Women with multiple husbands and divorces who are cohabiting with someone not their spouse can be found in every large city today and in many small towns as well. Yes, Jesus' recounting of her multiple failed marriages surprises her, for how could a stranger know such detail? But He offers no censure, only affirmation: "You are right. . . . What you have said is quite true." He offers her living water, though He has nothing to draw it with; He admits to being One greater than Jacob; somehow He knows about her failed relationships with men, and He does not condemn her! Her relief must be almost overwhelming. She feels safer with this all-seeing Jewish man than she has ever felt with anyone. How do we know? Because she has a question she has never dared ask anyone, and she asks it now.

" 'Sir,' the woman said, 'I can see that you are a prophet. Our ancestors worshiped on this mountain, but you Jews claim that the place where we must worship is in Jerusalem' " (verses 19, 20).

Understand, in those days very few ever changed their religion, because it was tied up with family, with ethnicity, and with loyalty to one's people and nation. Besides, who else would have her? Her Samaritan neighbors despised her. How much more would they hate her if she converted to Judaism? And as a Samaritan woman without a husband, virtually all Jews would scorn her interest in their religion, both because she was Samaritan and because she was disgraced.

But apparently she has always wondered, *Does the mountain you worship on make such a difference?* Again, both Samaritans and Jews would have reviled her for even thinking such a thing. But here she had found a prophet who could see her for who she was, for what she aspired to be, rather than whose daughter she was and how many men had rejected her. Here was her one chance to ask the question that had been bothering her. And Jesus' answer speaks to the deepest desires of her heart.

" 'Woman,' Jesus replied, 'believe me, a time is coming when you will worship the Father neither on this mountain nor in Jerusalem. You Samaritans worship what you do not know; we worship what we do know, for salvation is from the Jews. Yet a time is coming and has now come when the true worshipers will worship the Father in the Spirit and in truth, for they are the kind of worshipers the Father seeks. God is spirit, and His worshipers must worship in the Spirit and in truth' " (verses 21–24).

His answer to her? "You get it. The time will come when mountains don't matter." To the extent they do matter, the Samaritans are confused (worship what they do not know), and the Jews are correct (worship what we know; salvation is from the Jews). "But soon, and in fact, already, it's people just like you that God is looking for. People who understand that God is a spirit, know that He is not chained to one mountain or another. He wants people who understand that and worship Him for who He is!"

It must've been the answer she was seeking. Still, it seems so large, so sweeping, so inclusive, so alien to the cultures she knows, it's hard to take it all in. She senses in this stranger a wisdom beyond this world, even beyond that of the prophets. The vision of God He has shared with her awes her, humbles her. She loves it but realizes she cannot comprehend it all. She needs help of the kind only one person can give.

"The woman said, 'I know that Messiah (called Christ) is coming. When he comes, he will explain everything to us' " (verse 25).

In some ways, the next words Jesus utters are the most astonishing declaration in all the Gospels.

"Then Jesus declared, 'I who speak to you am he' " (verse 26).

In all the Gospels, this is the only time He explicitly makes this claim. At His trial, when the high priest demands to know if He is the Son of God, Jesus replies, "It is as you have said." When He read in the synagogue from Isaiah 61, He concludes by saying, "Today this was fulfilled in your hearing," from which His audience could infer that He was the Messiah. But only here, to this Samaritan woman with a tarnished reputation, does He openly declare rather than merely acknowledge His identity.

And this becomes even more remarkable when we compare this episode with the one that preceded it, the encounter with Nicodemus. Usually we see similarities between the spiritual woman in the story and some notable male character. But from the beginning, John's Gospel features dramatic contrasts: light and darkness, above and below, heaven and earth, the already and the not yet. And so it is with the woman at the well and Nicodemus. We have already mentioned some of these.

If we were primarily interested in Nicodemus, we could say much more about his encounter with Jesus. But we are focused on the Woman at the Well, and Nicodemus serves mainly as contrast. And what a contrast he provides!

Nicodemus is a Jewish leader. The Jews were to be a "light unto the nations."[1] So here comes this leader of the "light" to the One who *is* the Light—and he is *in the dark!* After verbally sparring with Jesus, he leaves in darkness, both literal and spiritual. The last words Jesus says to him are:

"This is the verdict: Light has come into the world, but people loved darkness instead of light because their deeds were evil. Everyone who does evil hates the light, and will not come into the light for fear that their deeds will be exposed. But whoever lives by the truth comes into the light, so that it may be seen plainly that what they have done has been done in the sight of God" (John 3:19–21).

This is the verdict? What a condemnation! Nicodemus came to Jesus in darkness, and Jesus tells him that those who do evil *will not come into the light!*

This explains why John made certain to tell us that the encounter with the Woman at the Well came "about noon." Although the Jews would have seen her, especially with her troubled marital history, as a child of darkness, she "comes into the light," both literally and spiritually, because she believes in Jesus as the Messiah!

The account of the Woman at the Well would be remarkable enough on its own, but John contrasted her with Jewish leader Nicodemus to demonstrate unmistakably the deep humility and great faith of this Gentile woman.

We're almost done, but we have two loose ends to tie up. First, we left the Betrothal Narrative unfinished. After talking with Jesus at the well, she rushes home to tell of this stranger.

"Then, leaving her water jar, the woman went back to the town and said to the people, 'Come, see a man who told me everything I ever did. Could this be the Messiah?' "(John 4:29).

So far so good. But what about the last two stages? The stranger is invited to share a meal, after which a betrothal takes place.

Interestingly, as soon as the woman goes back to the town:

Meanwhile his disciples urged him, "Rabbi, eat something."

But he said to them, "I have food to eat that you know nothing about."

Then his disciples said to each other, "Could someone have brought him food?"

"My food," said Jesus, is to do the will of him who sent me and to finish his work" (verses 32–34).

As we have come to expect, step six of the Betrothal Narrative occurs, but with a twist. Jesus refers to a *spiritual* repast rather than a physical one. And finally, there is step 7, betrothal. Does that happen? Clearly the woman believes, because her belief convinces others to seek Jesus. In the Old Testament, God says Israel is His bride; in the New Testament—specifically in Revelation, also written by John—spiritual Israel, or the church, is the Bride of Christ. Is it too great a stretch to conclude that since the Samaritan woman believes, she becomes part of the Bride? I'll leave that to you to decide.

And then we come to the question of whose "strong partner" this woman might be. She took the lead by taking the good news of the Messiah to her hometown, inhabited by Gentiles, with excellent results:

"Many of the Samaritans from that town believed in him because of the woman's testimony. . . . So when the Samaritans came to him, they urged him to stay with them, and he stayed two days. And because of his words many more became believers" (verses 39–41).

This woman functioned as an apostle to the Gentiles, the role the apostle Paul would later take on, making Paul her "strong partner." And note another contrast: Nicodemus did not remain with Jesus through the night, but because of the woman's testimony, Jesus remained with the Gentiles *two whole days.*

The Woman at the Well, contrasted with Nicodemus, dramatically illustrates one of the main themes of John's Gospel: "He came to that which was his own, but his own did not receive him. Yet to all who did receive him, to those who believed in his name, he gave the right to become children of God" (John 1:11, 12).

Eventually Nicodemus came to embrace Jesus as Messiah. But in chapter 3, Nicodemus, a Jew, one of God's "own," did not receive Him. The Woman at the Well—though a Gentile, a Samaritan, and an outcast even among the Samaritans—did.

---

1. See Isaiah 42:6; 49:6; 60:3.

FOURTEEN

THE BLEEDING WOMAN
FROM RAGS TO RIGHTEOUSNESS

There are some afflictions so intimate and so humbling that we dread to speak of them. And we all have them.

"Just then a woman who had been subject to bleeding for twelve years came up behind him and touched the edge of his cloak" (Matthew 9:20).

Bleeding for twelve years. We all know what this refers to, but we don't usually talk about it in polite company. When telling this story to children, we don't dwell on her malady. And that's appropriate, for children. But this is a story for adults. Of course, it would be easy to just skip over the distasteful parts of the Bible and make breezy statements about grace or healing. I don't know about you, but when I'm really struggling, I don't want blithe statements. I want comfort as deep as my despair and healing for my most painful wounds.

When we do speak of this woman's malady, we usually employ euphemisms like "feminine bleeding," and even that makes us feel uncomfortable and embarrassed. If you feel those emotions, then you are just beginning to understand this woman's plight. To really understand her story, we need to move past discomfort and embarrassment and move on to shame and despair. "But there's no shame in being ill," you may object. Really? Have you never been shamed, or felt ashamed, for being ill? Sometimes that's part of the illness.

Consider this poor woman's state of mind and body. To begin with, we need to recognize the sheer physical drain this placed on her. A twenty-first-century woman wrote a blog about her similar ordeal in these terms: "Blood loss . . . leave[s] us physically and spiritually weak, frail, anemic, haggard, overwhelmed, and fragile."[1]

THE BLEEDING WOMAN

"Weak, frail, anemic, haggard, overwhelmed, and fragile." No doubt twelve years of continuous blood loss would leave anyone feeling fragile, both physically and emotionally. But that's just the beginning of her suffering. Because of the continuous hemorrhaging, she was ritually unclean, making anyone or anything she touched unclean as well. This made her, at best, an object of pity, at worst an outcast, an object of revulsion to many—for twelve years.

Think of where you were and what was happening to you twelve years ago. Imagine that people had treated you as an outcast for twelve years. How would you feel? For twelve years, people shunned the woman, not wanting to be contaminated by her touch. How could this not impact her emotionally?

What about spiritual comfort? Forget it. Being ritually unclean prohibited her from going to the temple. If the crowds, even in the city streets, knew of her condition, they would draw away from her in horror. From virtually every source, she received the same message: You're tainted, you're defective, you're unclean, and you're repulsive.

If you think these ideas are a thing of the past or overstated, then be thankful you have not experienced them. Even today, people recoil at some diseases and conditions. I know of a couple whose child developed a particularly virulent cancer before his second birthday. Earnest church members felt obliged to tell these dear people that the child developed this terrible malignancy because of the parents' improper diet. (Physicians assured the couple that diet had nothing to do with the child's illness.) Similarly, obesity in our modern culture increasingly carries a stigma. Being shamed for physical conditions still goes on.

So this poor woman, in a state of chronic exhaustion, feeling overwhelmed and fragile due to continual blood loss, must also bear the burden of being shunned and reviled. She must have felt soiled down to the marrow of her bones.

This is a very short story, and each of the three synoptic Gospels includes slightly different details. To get the whole story, we shall have to include parts of all three accounts.

Interestingly, none of the three Gospels supplies us with her name, but this actually gives the story more meaning. As we examine her closely, we see she is every human—trying to become whole. Or, put another way, all of us are like her. As the prophet Isaiah said, "All of us have become like one who is unclean, and all our righteous acts are like filthy rags" (Isaiah 64:6).

This passage in Isaiah links each of us to the poor woman, because the Hebrew words translated "filthy rags" refer specifically to "used menstrual rags." First-century Jews certainly knew of this meaning. And if we make this connection with our short story, it reveals a new level of significance.

Now, we don't like to talk about menstrual rags. But this woman is deeply, movingly human. Her malady is a deeply human malady.

And, short as it is, the story makes clear that she has done everything in her power to find a cure. It's interesting to see the differences in the accounts about this. Mark tells us, "She had suffered a great deal under the care of many doctors and had spent all she had, yet instead of getting better she grew worse" (Mark 5:26). Perhaps out of professional courtesy, Luke, the physician, simply says "no one could heal her" (Luke 8:43).

She yearns to be whole. It is not a lack of desire for healing that keeps her hemorrhaging or that keeps her ritually unclean. Neither is it a lack of effort, but her efforts only result in a continual supply of filthy rags. Each of us shares her fate. We may greatly desire to be righteous, but we lack the power, and our attempts at righteousness only produce filthy rags, and leave us weak frail, anemic, haggard, overwhelmed, and fragile. According to Mark, this conscientious woman had consulted—and apparently paid—"many doctors." In our efforts to be righteous, we may consult with many spiritual gurus, pastors, or counselors. All these can be useful and helpful, but no matter how carefully we follow their advice, we cannot become righteous. Like the woman with the issue of blood, some of these prescriptions may actually make us worse, may convince us that we're becoming righteous, which, of course, only makes our true condition more serious.

She has tried everything, exhausted her financial resources, only to see her condition worsen. With all this, it wouldn't be surprising if she felt cursed by God Himself. But the coming of Jesus has brought her hope. She has heard of the miracles He has performed and has come to trust in His power. She brings no payment—she has none. She offers nothing—in her unclean state, she can provide nothing. She brings only her faith. She touches only the hem of His garment—the merest brush, the slightest contact. "She said to herself, 'If I only touch his cloak, I will be healed' " (Matthew 9:21).

The crowd has been jostling, pushing, prodding. People seeking, demanding Jesus' attention. He barely notices them. But the slightest touch of a trusting one seeking grace and the spark of divine power leaps from Him, suffusing her whole being with healing. This, too, demonstrates a deep spiritual truth. The purity of Christ eliminates impurity. That's true in our lives as well. That doesn't mean that we become instantly sinless. But the longer we allow Christ to sit on the throne of our hearts and the longer we stay in touch with Him, so to speak, the more His purity drives out our impurity; the more His holiness suffuses our lives and helps us to become holy.

" 'Who touched me?' Jesus asked. When they all denied it, Peter said, 'Master, the people are crowding and pressing against you.' But Jesus said, 'Someone touched me; I know that power has gone out from me' " (Luke 8:45, 46).

As often happens in the Gospels, Peter speaks, representing all of the twelve. And here Peter is incredulous. "You've got to be kidding," we can almost hear him say. "We're being jostled on every side by this crowd, and You want to know 'who touched you'? *Everybody touched You!*"

In this story Peter speaks for all who are spiritually unaware. I know, Peter is one of the inner circle. Ask anybody who knows anything about the New Testament what are the names of the disciples closest to Jesus, and they'll reply, "Peter, James, and John." But here he's clueless. At this moment, he's spiritually unaware. Not because spiritual things don't matter to him, but rather because he's focused on the logistics of getting Jesus safely from one place to another. That's not a foolish or sinful focus, it's a practical one—Peter's mind is focused on an urgent matter. Before the woman came into the story, Jesus had met someone else in great need:

"One of the synagogue leaders, named Jairus, came, and when he saw Jesus, he fell at his feet. He pleaded earnestly with him, 'My little daughter is dying. Please come and put your hands on her so that she will be healed and live.' So Jesus went with him" (Mark 5:22–24).

No wonder Peter is preoccupied. A desperately ill little girl lies close to death. That makes his incredulity at Jesus' words seem more reasonable. The group is on the way to save a little girl's life. Peter doesn't want to get there too late. So when Jesus stops and says, "Who touched me?" Peter may well have been thinking, *A little girl lies near death, and You want to know who touched You? Where are Your priorities? We need to get to that little girl before it's too late.* At least, that's what I would have thought. How about you?

But then Peter didn't know what Jesus knew, and what we know, having read the entire story—there is no such thing as "too late" for Jesus. In fact, all three Gospel accounts agree that even though the girl died before Jesus arrived in her home, it was not too late. He raised her from the dead. But that's another story, for another time.

In the press of events at this moment, we're with Peter, wondering how Jesus can ask, "Who touched Me?" That's because we don't actually understand Jesus' question. He's not unaware of being jostled, of being pushed, of people seeking, even demanding, His attention. And strangely enough, we know that the hemorrhaging woman barely touched the hem of His cloak. Jesus, like His Father, remains unmoved by efforts to push or force Him. The whirlwind, the earthquake, and the fire do not distract Him. But He always responds to the trusting heart, always hears the still, small voice—or even the unspoken cry—for help.

Jesus felt the power of God flowing out of Him, and He refused to let the incident pass unnoted. Mark tells us: "But Jesus kept looking around to see who had done it. Then the woman, knowing what had happened to her, came and fell at His feet and, trembling with fear, told Him the whole truth" (Mark 5:32, 33).

"Knowing what happened to her." The crowd knew nothing, Peter was unaware, but Jesus and the woman both knew what had happened. That's the thing about true faith, about truly trusting in God. You know. No one else may be able to see the change. And it may be in such a personal, private way that it cannot be detected by the casual observer. Still, the change is real.

At the same time, she realized that, according to custom, she had done something both forbidden and outrageous. Ritually unclean, she intentionally came into contact with someone who was ritually pure, and without His knowledge. So she confesses, as it says, "trembling with fear," and "told him the whole truth" (verse 33). She cannot truthfully say she is sorry, and yet, in her mind, it's almost as if she has stolen something, as if she took something that does not belong to her.

And Luke says: "In the presence of all the people, she told why she had touched him and how she had been instantly healed" (Luke 8:47).

She has confessed the "theft" and wonders what the penalty might be. Would her healing be revoked? Would she be stricken with something worse? In fact, she has nothing to worry about. Jesus lives to bless. He is eager to heal. She cannot take from God what He is not willing to give. So Jesus reassures her.

"Daughter, your faith has healed you. Go in peace and be freed from your suffering" (Mark 5:34).

There are few terms of endearment that evoke more tenderness than "son" or "daughter." "Daughter," Jesus says, setting her mind at rest, "your faith has healed you." As we noted before, God is so eager to give us healing that the merest touch of faith grants access to His healing power.

As far as her infraction of the rules is concerned, He says, "Go in peace." Modern translation: No problem. We're cool. It's fine. And then He adds the final benediction: *And be freed from your suffering.*

So this tiny gem of a story comes to a conclusion. What this unnamed woman accomplished defies comparison. We have many cases in Scripture, and indeed in our own lives, where someone prayed for a specific blessing and received it. We know that God desires to bless us. But here we see something different. Jesus appears not to know who touched Him. He appears not to have made a conscious choice to heal her. In other healings He has touched someone or molded clay with His own hands, or at least said something like, "Take up your bed and walk." Here He says nothing until *after* the healing occurs. "Someone touched me," He said. "I know that power has gone out from me" (Luke 8:46). The verbs are *past tense*. The touch has happened, and power flowed from Him—apparently without His conscious choice for it to occur.

What this tells us is almost beyond comprehension. God is so eager to bless and heal us that it is His default response, that is to say, healing and blessing us are the result—if such a thing is possible—automatically, without His volition, without His thinking about it. All we have to do is be willing to receive it. It's like when something gets close enough to high-voltage electrical lines, the surging current leaps the remaining gap, and a giant spark follows as the electricity goes to ground. Sometimes people ask if God is willing to forgive us, to save us, to heal us. This incident tells us that when faith reaches out to God, divine healing and salvation flow to faith and trust as surely and as automatically as electricity seeks the ground. When we reach out in faith to God, we unleash that mighty power in our lives!

There's no comparable event in Scripture. This unknown, never named, unfortunate, frail, ritually unclean, bleeding woman reached out, and in so doing revealed the amazing power of faith, the unlimited availability of divine power, as no one else ever did. The closest match I can think of for this anonymous sufferer is Job. Just as the story of his trials disclosed a truth about the conflict between Christ and Satan that we find nowhere else, her act of faith uncovered something about Jesus that could be revealed in no other way. The stories of Job and the bleeding woman add to our understanding of God some information that we would not have imagined, could not have made up. And that is why they are included in Scripture.

As Paul said, *"Oh the depth of the riches both of the wisdom and the knowledge of God! How unsearchable are his judgments, and his ways past tracing out!"* (Romans 11:33, WEB; emphasis added).

This story demonstrates both that God's ways truly are "past tracing out" and that He is eager that we should understand Him and His unfathomable love for us.

---

1. John Garr, "The Hem of His Garment: A Hebraic Perspective," *Heart of Wisdom: Bible Based Homeschooling*, accessed January 25, 2017, http://heartofwisdom.com/blog/the-woman-with-the-issue-of-blood/.

FIFTEEN

THE SYROPHOENICIAN WOMAN
Wit and Tenacity

Despite His best efforts to stay out of sight, she discovered that He was hiding out in a private home nearby. Greek herself, living in Syrian Phoenicia, she nonetheless determined to seek help for her daughter from the Jewish teacher.

"Jesus left that place and went to the vicinity of Tyre. He entered a house and did not want anyone to know it; yet he could not keep his presence secret. In fact, as soon as she heard about him, a woman whose little daughter was possessed by an impure spirit came and fell at his feet. The woman was a Greek, born in Syrian Phoenicia" (Mark 7:24–28).

This episode is described in both Matthew and Mark in the same context: Jesus had just had an encounter with the Pharisees in Jerusalem over ceremonial uncleanliness. At least in partial response, He withdrew northward through Galilee, into Phoenicia. His reputation preceded Him, and this Gentile—and therefore "unclean"—woman was seeking His help.

Some modern commentators see what follows in this episode as evidence that Jesus Himself possessed ethnic prejudice. However, let's look at the text again, keeping in mind the context: the previous episode in the narrative is a conflict between Jesus and the Pharisees over what makes a person unclean. Here comes an "unclean" woman.

" 'Lord, Son of David, have mercy on me! My daughter is demon-possessed and suffering terribly.' Jesus did not answer a word. So his disciples came to him and urged him, 'Send her away, for she keeps crying out after us' " (Matthew 15:22, 23).

Jesus did not answer a word. He did not utter an ethnic slur. Why His silence?

Because He realizes His disciples have not absorbed the lesson from the previous episode, namely, that spiritual "uncleanness" is not about things outside—ethnicity or hygiene or diet—but about what is within, that which "comes out of a person." He had to explain it several ways, and the disciples still did not get it. So here's a real-life example. That's why He did not answer a word to the woman.

Rather than tell the disciples what to think, He waited for them to speak, to reveal what was in their hearts. For them, this Gentile woman was an annoyance, and they told Him to send her away. But He does not. They see her as a Gentile; He sees that she possesses great faith. In fact, given that she understands how the typical Jew of her day regards her, it has taken significant courage—fueled by faith and need—for her even to approach Him. But of course, there were always those who sought Him because of His fame rather than faith. So He proceeds to test both her and His disciples.

"He answered, 'I was sent only to the lost sheep of Israel' " (Matthew 15:24).

This is not an ethnic slur, though it could be interpreted as one. When Jesus sent the disciples out in Matthew 10, it was "with the following instructions: 'Do not go among the Gentiles or enter any town of the Samaritans. Go rather to the lost sheep of Israel' " (Matthew 10:5, 6).

Jesus' ministry begins with Israel, because judgment will begin with them (see 1 Peter 4:17), so this statement describes the focus of His ministry, not the limit or extent of it. But it could be understood as "You're not included," which would have matched the understanding of both the disciples and the woman. She may well have expected it. In any case, it did not deter her.

"The woman came and knelt before him. 'Lord, help me!' she said. He replied, 'It is not right to take the children's bread and toss it to the dogs' " (Matthew 15:25, 26).

No doubt the disciples agreed with equating Gentiles with dogs. Since dogs scavenged, eating all sorts of dead and decaying animals, they were considered ceremonially unclean—as were the Gentiles. But the woman remained resolute, even after this stinging rebuke.

" 'Yes it is, Lord,' she said. 'Even the dogs eat the crumbs that fall from their master's table' " (verse 27).

She handles this third rebuke with wit and humility. She doesn't mind being called a dog if it means help for her suffering child. Whether this display of character rebuked the disciples, we are not told. But Jesus can no longer hold up the pretense; He cannot prolong her disappointment.

"Then Jesus said to her, 'Woman, you have great faith! Your request is granted.' And her daughter was healed at that moment" (verse 28).

That's the end of this brief episode. We do not hear of this woman or her daughter again. Yet she left a significant impression. Hearing of Jesus' presence nearby, well aware of the censure she might encounter, she nonetheless took the initiative to seek Him out. Having found Him, she did not let His silence, or the scorn of His disciples, or His repeated apparent rebukes dissuade her.

There is no textual link between this episode and anything in the Old Testament, but it brings to my mind the image of Jacob, wrestling with the Angel all night, and even after painful injury, vowing not to let go without a blessing. For that, he earned the name Israel, for he struggled and prevailed. And so, this unnamed Greek woman from Phoenicia verbally wrestled with the Savior, and she prevailed as well.

SIXTEEN

Mary of Bethany
The Fragrance of Devotion

Mary *knew*. Jesus had told His disciples more than once, but when the immediate crisis passed, they forgot. But Mary knew. She could hear it in Jesus' words, see it in His face; and she could feel it when in the presence of Pharisees or priests. His enemies lay in wait, and they would not wait much longer. Her emotions, raw from grieving her brother's death, then celebrating his return from the dead, now turned to grief and dread for what she saw ahead, and now, the darkness seemed to close in on every side. She could not prevent the terrible events, could not even slow their approach. But she must do something.

"Six days before the Passover, Jesus came to Bethany, where Lazarus lived, whom Jesus had raised from the dead. Here a dinner was given in Jesus' honor. Martha served, while Lazarus was among those reclining at the table with him" (John 12:1, 2).

Six days before the Passover. In a scant two weeks, Jesus will be betrayed, flogged, crucified, buried, and then rise again. He, the Lamb of God, undoubtedly knows how short is the time before His sacrifice. Mary of Bethany, sister to Martha and Lazarus, does not know. But she is so attuned to Jesus that she senses something ominous.

Not long before, her brother Lazarus had lain on his death bed. Jesus, in faraway Galilee, heard of the illness and announced His intention to come to Judea, to Bethany. During His previous trip to Judea, the Jews had tried to stone Him. His disciples reminded Him of the danger, but He resolved to go anyway.

Apparently, He arrived four days too late—or so it seemed—for Lazarus had died and was buried before Jesus' arrival. And then—and then—it still staggered Mary's imagination to recall what He had done. He had gone to Lazarus' tomb and called to her brother to come out—and he came!

She had gone from bitter tears to grateful ones, astonished ones. Now, today, the two men she loved most sat at dinner together, talking and laughing, enjoying life to the full. Yet she sensed they were both surrounded by danger. Martha coped with the wild emotional swings the way she coped with everything—busying herself with housework. If she saw what loomed in the future, she didn't show it. But Mary saw and decided to do the only thing she knew to express her gratitude for restoring her brother, for the beautiful truths He shared about His Father, for the love He radiated continuously, and for the peril He faced.

"Then Mary took about a pint of pure nard, an expensive perfume; she poured it on Jesus' feet and wiped his feet with her hair. And the house was filled with the fragrance of the perfume" (verse 3).

Nard is a variety of lavender, so we can imagine the fragrance. And imagine sixteen ounces of lavender poured out in a short time! No wonder the house was filled with its fragrance. Like Jesus' life and ministry, it was healing and sweet and restful—and bound to attract attention.

"But one of his disciples, Judas Iscariot, who was later to betray him, objected, 'Why wasn't this perfume sold and the money given to the poor? It was worth a year's wages' " (verses 4, 5).

So much was conveyed in those twenty-two words. Unmoved by her tears, by her worshipful wiping of Jesus' feet with her hair, Judas—who, John reminds us, will later betray Jesus—criticizes her action. Financier J. P. Morgan, experienced in dealing with people seeking money, said, "A man always has two reasons for doing anything: a good reason and the real reason." It may not always be true, but here it certainly is. Judas objects that the money—a year's income—might have been spent on the poor. That was his good reason. John informs us of the real reason.

"He did not say this because he cared about the poor but because he was a thief; as keeper of the money bag, he used to help himself to what was put into it" (verse 6).

Oscar Wilde described a cynic as "a man who knows the price of everything, and the value of nothing." This is an apt description of Judas here. Focused on money, Judas is blind to the larger reality, oblivious to his own motives, and to the tragic part he will soon play in this cosmic drama. What a contrast! An act of amazing devotion and love from one who sees Jesus' peril, opposed by the very man who will seal Jesus' capture and execution!

This should serve as a cautionary tale for today. We live in a culture of "Compassion Pharisees," where many who proclaim their concern for the poor and suffering in the public square do so like Judas, as cover for their own greed or their appetite for power. The words sound good, but then so did those of the Pharisees in Jesus' day.

But Jesus can read hearts.

" 'Leave her alone,' Jesus replied. 'It was intended that she should save this perfume for the day of my burial. You will always have the poor among you, but you will not always have me' " (verse 7).

This explains it all. For some time, Jesus has been telling the disciples that He must soon die. But because it does not match their expectations for the Messiah, they fail to comprehend that the time is rapidly approaching. Mary has also heard, and though she may not have understood everything, she understood enough.

"Meanwhile a large crowd of Jews found out that Jesus was there and came, not only because of him but also to see Lazarus, whom he had raised from the dead. So the chief priests made plans to kill Lazarus as well, for on account of him many of the Jews were going over to Jesus and believing in him" (verses 9–11).

We cannot say for certain that she knew of these plans. But her actions in this episode suggest that she sensed the crisis looming, the menace both to her brother and to her Lord. Jesus says directly that the perfume had been intended for His burial. It appears she wanted to express her love and sympathy for Jesus while He yet lived, perhaps to tell Him she saw what was coming, as an encouragement that His approaching sacrifice would not be unappreciated.

As we saw with the Woman at the Well, John's gospel often focuses on contrasts, and in this episode, Mary's foresight, faith, and love contrast drastically with the blind greed of Judas and the murderous intent of the Jewish leadership. Mary of Bethany and Judas both believed in Jesus' great power, but they reacted in drastically different ways. Judas shared the idea of Jesus as leader against the corrupt power structure in Jerusalem, Jewish as well as Roman. He thought Jesus needed a little nudge to get Him to exercise His power. That's clear from his reaction when he realized Jesus would allow Himself to be crucified. Matthew tells us, "When Judas, who had betrayed him, saw that Jesus was condemned, he was seized with remorse and returned the thirty pieces of silver to the chief priests and the elders. 'I have sinned,' he said, 'for I have betrayed innocent blood' " (Matthew 27:3, 4).

"When he saw that Jesus was condemned . . ." Well, what had he expected? Everyone knew the Jewish leaders had been plotting to kill Jesus for months. Judas betrayed Jesus into their hands, and they condemned Him. Again I ask, "What did he expect?" The answer clearly is—*something else!* It seems likely he expected Jesus to assert His power and authority to escape capture. Judas perhaps saw his action as a catalyst to start a revolution.

Among those close to Jesus, Mary alone appears to have absorbed His teaching and had a glimpse of His true mission. She alone took the initiative to bring Him comfort in the days just before His greatest trial.

In both the Old and New Testaments, incense in the temple represents the prayers of the saints. Here, in a private home in Bethany, the fragrance of perfume, and of Mary's devotion, "filled the house." And whenever this story is told, that wonderful scent lingers to this day.

SEVENTEEN

Mary of Magdala
Apostle to the Apostles

Probably more has been written about Mary of Magdala than any other woman in Scripture, with the possible exception of Mary the mother of Jesus. There are so many stories, so many ideas about Mary in circulation that it would be difficult to even survey them all. On one extreme, she's considered to have been a prostitute. On the other—sometimes by the same people—she is thought to be the wife of Jesus. But of course the latter is not true. Whether or not she was a prostitute is not so simple.

For all the speculation about her, we really know very little. Scripture does state directly that Jesus cast seven demons out of her. But precisely how that demon possession manifested itself, we do not know, as we are not told. Magdala, the town from which Mary came and from which she derived her surname, was a fishing town on the shores of Galilee. Archeologists have determined that fish provided the major source of protein for many Jews in Jesus' day. Fish caught in the lake were salted and dried in Magdala and then transported elsewhere. Many, of course, went to Jerusalem.

Like sailors everywhere, fishermen were known for their appetites, including sexual ones. Towns filled with sailors, then as now, attracted a number of women whose only means of supporting themselves was to sell their bodies. Possibly, as is all too common today, some young girls were trafficked there and suffered significant trauma. If Mary of Magdala was one of these, it might well explain her symptoms. Still, we do not know. Scripture is silent on the matter.

But since the town had that reputation in those days, many people may have assumed she was a prostitute simply because she came from there. Don't forget,

Nathaniel's question in John 1:46. "Nazareth! Can anything good come from there?" reminds us that Nazareth also had a bad reputation, though perhaps of a different sort.

What we see in Mary is a woman continually anticipating Jesus' needs and providing for them.

"After this, Jesus traveled about from one town and village to another, proclaiming the good news of the kingdom of God. The Twelve were with him, and also some women who had been cured of evil spirits and diseases: Mary (called Magdalene) from whom seven demons had come out; Joanna the wife of Chuza, the manager of Herod's household; Susanna; and many others. These women were helping to support them out of their own means" (Luke 8:1–3).

This is pretty much all we know of Mary of Magdala—until the Crucifixion. The Gospels all agree that Mary of Magdala was there, although Luke simply refers to "the women who had followed him from Galilee" (Luke 23:49). In other words, the women he told us about in chapter 8.

The synoptic Gospels tell us that Mary accompanied His body to the tomb. Though the four Gospels differ in detail about how many and which women went to Jesus' tomb on Resurrection morning, the only one they all place there is Mary Magdalene. She went because Jesus' body had been taken to the tomb just before the Sabbath, and they had not had time to fully prepare it by anointing it with spices. Once there, she discovered the stone had been rolled away from the entrance and the tomb was empty. And she received this commission from an angelic being:

" 'Don't be alarmed,' he said. 'You are looking for Jesus the Nazarene, who was crucified. He has risen! He is not here. See the place where they laid him. But go, tell his disciples and Peter, "He is going ahead of you into Galilee. There you will see him, just as he told you" ' " (Mark 16:6, 7).

This passage gives rise to calling Mary Magdalene the "apostle to the apostles." "Go, tell" is the essence of the apostolic commission. She is to go and take the very good news of Jesus' resurrection to all the male disciples. "Tell his disciples and Peter . . ." These five words say a great deal. Throughout the Gospels, Peter speaks as the representative of the Twelve, and he is sometimes tasked with communicating Jesus' will to the others. But here, even he will be informed by Mary.

As an added irony, scholars generally agree that the source of Mark's Gospel was Peter. It's possible that Peter, remembering his denial of Jesus, placed himself last in this account as an act of humility. It is also possible that the angel wanted to make certain that Peter realized that Jesus still considered him one of the Twelve, and singled him out to make sure he would be informed.

What we see in Mary of Magdala is someone relentlessly conscientious in ministry to Jesus, even to death and beyond. Most of the time, her actions attract little or no attention. That matters little to her. She continually shows initiative in the mundane and sometimes distasteful chores of life. After all, when last seen in the Bible, she goes to anoint a dead body. In the normal course of events, it would not have been either noticed or mentioned, like the rest of her ministry.

Except for the lower status of women in first-century Judaism, we should not be surprised that Mary received the high honor of being the apostle to the apostles, the first human to proclaim the resurrection of Christ. For Jesus had said, "Whoever can be trusted with very little can also be trusted with much" (Luke 16:10). She was continually faithful in the small tasks, and so God gave her one of greatest tasks of all time—and made sure the men who wrote the Gospels included it!

EIGHTEEN

WHAT THESE STORIES HAVE TAUGHT ME

From the age of twelve I had to wear eyeglasses. Quite nearsighted, and with astigmatism as well, for the next half-century or so I had to wear glasses almost every waking hour in order to function effectively. Then, several years ago, I developed cataracts. The one in my left eye, particularly, was so large and so dense that when I took the eye exam for my driver's license, I could see light with that eye, but I could not identify a single letter. I was essentially blind in that eye.

The surgery, though I approached it with great trepidation, was uneventful. It took no more than fifteen minutes, and ten minutes after that, I walked out of the hospital under my own power. In addition to removing the cataract, the surgeon had inserted corrective lenses into my eyes, with the result that instead of my vision being 20/200, it was now 20/40. For the first time in my life, I got a driver's license that had no restrictions on it—I could drive without glasses. But the immediate effect after surgery was even more dramatic.

Up until that time, my world was either blurred or filtered through thick lenses. But suddenly I saw the world clearly without corrective lenses, and it took my breath away. Suddenly it was so deep, so three-dimensional. It was as though my glasses had been a poor-quality screen on which the world was projected, restricting and flattening everything. The surgery didn't just remove the milky white spot that blurred one eye, it literally changed the way I saw the world.

I mention that because this study of women who took the initiative in the Bible had a similar effect on me. It did not just change how I viewed women, or women in the Bible. It changed how I saw *all* of Scripture.

Of course, there are some similarities between the women in these stories and men of great faith. Shakespeare said that some men are born to greatness, some achieve greatness, and some have greatness thrust upon them. That seems an accurate description of the spiritual greatness of the women we have studied.

Deborah, Abigail, the Woman of Shunem, and Ruth are examples of women whose conduct is so noble from beginning to end that they appear born to greatness. They continually display a nobility of character rare in either sex—any time, any place. Every action, every word exhibits wisdom and honor.

Tamar, Hannah, Rahab, and the Syrophoenician woman are examples of women who, when confronted with difficult and challenging circumstances, respond with extraordinary effort and thus achieve remarkable things.

Esther, Bathsheba, and Mary the mother of Jesus appear to have greatness thrust upon them. Circumstances not of their choosing confront them with an opportunity—and a burden. Though they might have refused this unsought opportunity, they accepted and bore it with grace.

And that leads us to the answer of how God responds when women take the lead. He pours out His grace and approval on them according to their faith. It does not matter whether the male authorities in their life agree or approve; it does not matter whether their actions are socially acceptable; it does not matter their station in life—from social outcast or lowly peasant, to respectable matron or queen. It does not matter whether they have followed the correct doctrine or belong to the chosen people. It does not matter whether they appear devout, debauched, or drunk. It does not matter whether they are single, divorced, or widowed. When women take the initiative to act in faith, God rewards them, just as He does with men. But that was just the beginning.

For one thing, these stories stand in dramatic contrast to the notion that biblical writers were simply creatures of their time. It is increasingly common to write off portions of Scripture that we find disturbing as "culturally conditioned." It allows us to avoid dealing with passages that challenge our assumptions, or make us feel out of tune with the spirit of the times. These stories refute the one such popular perception, that the Bible is hostile to women.

While it is true that the *culture* in which these narratives were written did indeed relegate women to the status of property, the stories themselves leave no doubt as to the moral and spiritual significance of these women. The authors—all male—do not hesitate to demonstrate their heroine's achievements, moral insight, behavior, courage, intelligence, and leadership as equal or superior to those of the greatest men in Scripture. This stands out as one examines the stories in detail. And it's another testimony to the radical difference between the Bible and other ancient texts. Only the Bible significantly challenges the prejudices and flaws of the culture from which it arises.

And there is more. Even though the male authors were able to overcome the prejudices of their culture when writing about these remarkable women, there is one lack which they remained powerless to remedy. When Old Testament authors want us to know what a character thinks, they express it as internal dialog. When it comes to the male characters in the Bible stories, their motivation and internal struggles are noted. For example:

"Then Abraham fell on his face, and laughed, and *said in his heart*, 'Will a child be born to him who is one hundred years old? Will Sarah, who is ninety years old, give birth?' " (Genesis 17:17, WEB; emphasis added).

"Esau *said in his heart*, 'The days of mourning for my father are at hand. Then I will kill my brother Jacob' " (Genesis 27:41, WEB; emphasis added).

"Jeroboam *said in his heart,* 'Now the kingdom will return to David's house' " (1 Kings 12:26, WEB; emphasis added).

"Haman *said in his heart,* 'Who would the king delight to honor more than myself?' " (Esther 6:6, WEB; emphasis added).

There are more examples, but these show that the biblical authors revealed thoughts and motivations as what a man "says in his heart." But when it comes to women, only once in Scripture do we have the expression "said in *her* heart." When Hannah made her vow, she did not speak it aloud, only her lips moving, and because of this Eli mistakenly accused her of being drunk. So, even in this case, it is not her thoughts that are revealed but the silent words of her vow. The author needed the precise words of the vow for the story to make sense. Indeed, the wording of the vow would be recorded so that Hannah could verify that she had fulfilled it. So, however he obtained the words, they were in fact spoken words and not simply internal thoughts.

In other words, the female mind is effectively opaque to the male authors. Readers must deduce their motives and thoughts from their actions. In the story of Hannah, we know she is miserable because Penninah "provoked her severely, to irritate her" (1 Samuel 1:6, WEB). When Hannah weeps as a result, Elkanah personifies this male bafflement at female psychology by saying, pathetically, "Hannah, why do you weep? Why don't you eat? Why is your heart grieved? Am I not better to you than ten sons?" (1 Samuel 1:8, WEB). *Elkanah doesn't get it.*

We come closest to seeing a woman's internal thoughts when Michal sees David dancing, and the author tells us "she despised him in her heart" (1 Chronicles 15:29, WEB). Despising, however, is far from a subtle emotion and can easily be deduced from her subsequent actions and words. And it still leaves open the debate about precisely what inspired Michal's contempt. Was it because David was immodest, or because she thought it beneath his royal dignity to worship so enthusiastically? Even in this case, aside from the blatant display of the contempt in her heart, we are left wondering about Michal's internal thoughts.

WHAT THESE STORIES HAVE TAUGHT ME

In the story of David and Bathsheba, the author gives no indication as to what she thinks, and wants, and why she does what she does. The same is true of Vashti in the Esther story. She refuses the king's demand to come to his banquet, but that is all we are told. And in the New Testament, Luke—who, as a physician, gives the most details about Mary's pregnancy and remarks on Jesus' development as a child—still finds Mary opaque. When the shepherds testify concerning the angels' song at Jesus' birth, or when Jesus explains His three-day absence while teaching the rabbis, Luke tells us that Mary "kept these things in her heart," or "pondered them in her heart" (see Luke 2:19). On the content of those ponderings, he has nothing to offer.

This grants us another window into how inspiration works. Of course, God knows everyone's thoughts, and He knew the thoughts of these women. God knew, but the male writers didn't, and the text reflects their lack of knowledge. It also demonstrates that the lack of female authors deprives us of a perspective only they could have given.

Which leads me to a final discovery. Several of the stories about women in the Bible are ones that we tend to minimize or neglect because they involve topics that make us—specifically men—uncomfortable. They make us uncomfortable because they are things that circumstances generally do not force us to deal with: menstruation, childbirth, the aftermath and consequences of sex. Others involved menial chores such as drawing water from a well, laundering soiled and bloodied cloth, anointing a dead body. But women dealt with them—and still deal with some of these issues—on a routine basis, and often silently.

That's another reason the portrayal of women in Scripture is so important: it demonstrates that God is the God of blood, tears, toil, and grief; the God of prostitutes and those scorned as well as those whom society values. He is the God of the full spectrum of human experience from its most sublime to its most basic. To portray this fully, there must be stories about women because they experience the full spectrum of life: in menstruation, pregnancy, childbirth, and dirty diapers; in fertility and barrenness; in care giving and receiving; in rejection and neglect. And to express this fully to a hurting world requires women as well as men, because there are some ways in which only women can fully minister.

These stories not only defy the stereotypes of their culture, but they refute those of our time. In fact I increasingly realized that none of the standard approaches to women's role, in the past or in the contemporary culture, explained what I saw in Scripture. My reading identified three basic ideas about the role of women in contemporary culture, and in the church: egalitarian, self-styled progressive, and traditional.

The egalitarian position at first seems most credible. Yes, Scripture affirms that before God, men and women are equal. But in practice, using this approach, equality means *identical* and *interchangeable*. These stories demonstrate that men and women are indeed equal but far from identical and interchangeable. The story of Tamar, for example, only works at all because Tamar is a woman and Judah a man. As the story stands, Tamar emerges as intelligent and resourceful. Reversing the sexes of the two main characters would only result in a farce. The same treatment would render the stories of Rahab, Ruth, Bathsheba, and Esther either ridiculous or routine.

The problem with both the progressive and traditionalist approaches is that—whether they intend to or not—they tacitly promote a stereotype which these stories refute. Self-styled "progressives" promote the "professional woman" as the only way for a woman to reach "her full potential." They give lip service to the notion that being "just a mother" is acceptable, but even the phrase "*just* a mother" implies that the woman has settled for something less than she should, that she has failed to fulfill her true destiny. On the other side, defenders of what they see as "traditional values" promote the notion that not only is motherhood "the highest calling" in general for women, it is also "the highest calling" for each *particular* woman. For them, a woman who undertakes a profession—other than a few traditionally acceptable ones, like teacher or nurse—has chosen to neglect her "higher calling" to motherhood. Neither matches what we see in Scripture, nor does either of these views leave much room for individuality.

The Bible, on the other hand, celebrates and praises individual women for who they *are* and what they *do*, not for who they *might have been* or what else *they might have done*. A look back at the stories we have studied makes this clear.

We don't know if Deborah, for example, had any children at all. That's because she made a great individual contribution as a military leader and judge. Hannah's signal contribution to God's plan, on the other hand, comes out of her great desire to be a mother! Do we really think Israel would have benefited more if Hannah, having failed to have children, had put her energies into reaching "her full potential" trying to be a judge like Deborah? Then Samuel would never have existed!

Should teenage Mary have said, "I'm too young to have a child; it will stunt my development as a person"? Ruth, as we have seen, is a monumental figure of faith, but in human terms, many would consider her a disappointment, an example of wasted potential. We see her ministering to her mother-in-law, doing the most menial of tasks—gleaning—and eventually marrying an older man and . . . having a baby! And we could go on.

Most of the women in this study, though the biblical authors portray them as spiritual heroines, otherwise lived fairly unremarkable lives. The result of Tamar's extraordinary effort is that she becomes a mother of twins. Rahab, after saving Israel, has a baby named Boaz. Jochebed outwits Pharaoh to save her infant son. Ruth and Hannah become mothers. The Woman of Shunem, aside from her encounters with Elisha, has an ordinary life. The Woman at the Well, the bleeding woman, and the Syrophoenician woman live out their lives in anonymity. With few notable exceptions—Deborah, Rahab, and Esther—the deeds of these women are recorded for us not because they led armies, won battles, or influenced kings but precisely because, in the course of pursuing otherwise ordinary lives, they were instrumental in God's work.

What this tells us is that *there is no higher calling* than what God calls you to do. Man or woman, each of us has a unique role to play in God's plan. The record of Scripture, and specifically the stories we have examined, indicates that God calls whom He will, without regard to our categories and expectations. General rules and roles may have to bend for us to accomplish God's will for our life, because those roles and rules are general, and each of us is unique. After all, the God who makes each snowflake unique surely invest as much creativity in each of us.

At the same time, because the Bible stories are about particular individuals with different callings, we must be careful about promoting any one of them as a role model. Jesus is our Example, but that does not mean that we all should remain single as He did. Neither should all men go looking for a promiscuous prostitute to marry—but God called Hosea to do precisely that. Not every childless widow should seduce her father-in-law in order to conceive, as Tamar did. These are extremes, but they underline the lesson that God has a unique calling for each of us, and we should not concern ourselves too much with what God calls another to do or the expectations others have for us.. When it comes to that, we would do well to remember what Jesus pointed out to Peter. "If I want him to remain alive until I return, what is that to you? You must follow me" (John 21:22).

What was true for Peter is true for us. Man or woman, our calling is the same: to follow Him *wherever* He leads.